SPHERE RI

Series Edito

THE SEX DISCRIMINATION HANDBOOK

HARJIT GREWAL

SPHERE REFERENCE

A SPHERE BOOK

First published in Great Britain
by Sphere Books Ltd 1990

Typeset in Plantin by Leaper & Gard Ltd, Bristol, England
Printed and bound in Great Britain by
The Guernsey Press

ISBN 0-7474-0217-5

Sphere Books Ltd
A Division of
Macdonald & Co (Publishers) Ltd
27 Wrights Lane, London W8 5TZ
A member of Maxwell Pergamon Publishing Corporation plc

Publisher's Note

The law can change at short notice. This book describes the law on sex discrimination as at 31st July 1989. You should always check if what it says is still correct.

In this book the discriminator is generally referred to as male for reasons of clarity. Of course, discrimination is not only practised by men and it should be borne in mind that what is said also applies to female discriminators.

Equally, members of certain professions are usually referred to either as he or she. Once again, this is to facilitate easy reading.

Contents

Introduction

Two Acts of Parliament, passed relatively recently – the Sex Discrimination Act in 1975 and the Equal Pay Act in 1970 (but which only came into force in 1975) – have made discrimination against women unlawful in a variety of areas of their lives. Although it is generally known that sex discrimination is unlawful, it is not always clear what in law amounts to discrimination.

It is only rarely that discrimination is overt and can be spotted as such. Far more often what may appear on the face of it to be unobjectionable behaviour by someone is, if looked at closely, discriminatory and, therefore, unlawful.

The purpose of this book is twofold. First, it is to outline the kind of conduct which in law amounts to sex discrimination. It explains how certain requirements or conditions may be discriminatory, and how in certain circumstances it may be unlawful to discriminate against married persons, parents and pregnant women.

It is hoped that this will be useful in two respects. First, it should enable you to spot discrimination which may not be obvious, and, therefore, to take some action in respect of it. Secondly, it should provide some guidelines as to what action can be taken to prevent discrimination. In this context, trade unions may find it beneficial when negotiating with employers.

The book provides many examples of the type of conduct which may be unlawful sex discrimination in various spheres of your life, such as at work, in education, in housing and in the provision of goods, facilities and services. It is not, however, possible to formulate strict formulae which can provide an answer to every given problem. Whether or not you have been discriminated against will depend on the facts and all the surrounding circumstances of your individual case, and the interpretation placed on them by the industrial tribunal or the court.

It is important to remember that although the law is laid down in Acts of Parliament, the extent of its application to any given situation is determined by the tribunals and the courts. Thus the law is not static and frequently changes as certain decisions are reached or are reversed by the higher courts. This book can do no more than outline the kind of behaviour which may be unlawful, and alert you to the possibility that sex discrimination may be taking place.

The second purpose of this book is to provide some guidance as to what can be done once you are aware that discrimination has taken place. It is important to remember that there are fixed time limits within which any action can be taken. It is, therefore, imperative that you seek advice and institute proceedings as soon as possible.

This book provides the names and addresses of certain agencies which can provide you with legal assistance free of charge in situations where legal aid is not available. You may in certain circumstances decide to represent yourself or be represented by a non-legally qualified person in an industrial tribunal. This book explains in some detail how to prepare your case, the procedure at the tribunal and the proving of discrimination.

If you are legally represented, it is hoped that the book will assist you in preparing your case and in raising and discussing the relevant issues with your lawyers.

The main purpose of the book remains, however, to make you aware of your rights and to alert you to recognize discriminatory behaviour, so that you can stand up and fight for your rights.

1: The Meaning of Discrimination

What is discrimination?

Discrimination generally means treating someone less favourably than others. It can occur in one of two ways; it can be either 'direct' (see below) or 'indirect' (see page 5). You must not be discriminated against:

(a) because of your sex;

(b) in the field of employment (see chapters 2 and 3), because you are a married person; *or*

(c) by way of victimization (see page 13).

Can men complain of sex discrimination?

Yes. Discrimination against men is unlawful in exactly the same way as discrimination against women. The only difference is that men cannot complain of sex discrimination because they do not benefit from any special treatment that may be afforded to women in connection with pregnancy or childbirth.

In this book the persons referred to as being the victims of sex discrimination will generally be women. It should be borne in mind, however, that whatever is said in relation to them applies equally to men, except where pregnancy and birth benefits are concerned.

What is direct discrimination?

Direct discrimination is quite straightforward; it simply means that you are being treated less favourably than a man in a similar position to you is actually treated or would be treated, and the reason for it is that you are a woman.

Similarly, in the employment context, it is direct discrimination if you are treated less favourably than a single person in a similar position to you is actually treated or would be treated, and the reason for it is that you are a married person.

Two factors must be borne in mind. First, it does not matter if there is no actual man (or single person) with whom you can compare yourself. You can compare yourself with a hypothetical man (or single person). For instance, a woman is the only applicant for a job and she is refused the job. She can still allege sex discrimination even though there is no male applicant with whom she can compare herself. Second, the person with whom you compare yourself (either actual or hypothetical) must be someone in roughly the same position as yourself. Thus you cannot complain of sex discrimination if a man with longer experience and better qualifications than yourself is promoted instead of you.

Although it is easy to understand what direct discrimination means, it is quite another matter trying to prove it. Those who treat you less favourably on the grounds of your sex are hardly likely to admit that they have done so and, no doubt, will put forward other reasons for the less favourable treatment. In determining whether sex discrimination has taken place, courts and tribunals will look at all the circumstances, including the reasons put forward by the discriminator for the less favourable treatment, and see whether they can infer from these circumstances that an act of discrimination has taken place.

The following are examples of what may amount to direct discrimination:

You have worked for a particular company for many years. The post of regional manager becomes available and you have all the necessary qualifications for it. Instead of promoting you to that post, the company promotes a man whose qualifications are no better than yours and who has been with the company for only a few months.

You are in a wine bar and go up to the bar to buy a drink. You are told that only men can buy drinks at the bar; women have to remain seated and be served at their tables.

It is important to remember that if women are treated less favourably because of typical, traditional, general or stereotyped assumptions about their role in society, that can amount to sex discrimination. For instance, you marry a man who works for a competitor of the company for which you work. Both employers are unhappy about the situation. They get together and decide that you must be dismissed without anyone looking at your respective wages to see which of you earns more. That would be sex discrimination because it would be based on the assumption that men are more likely than women to be the primary supporters of their spouses and children.

Another example of sex discrimination based on stereotyped assumptions would be the refusal to offer a woman a job in London when it is learnt that her husband is due to be transferred to Leeds in six months' time. The refusal to offer her the job is based on the assumption that married women always follow their husbands, and that the couple will make their home where the husband has a job.

What is indirect discrimination?

Indirect discrimination is slightly more complicated. It takes place if someone imposes a 'requirement' or 'condition' which, on the face of it, has nothing to do with your sex and appears to apply equally to men and women, but which, in reality, is such that the proportion of women who can comply with it is considerably smaller than the proportion of men who can comply with it. If there is no justification for it and you are adversely affected by it because you cannot comply with it, then it is indirect discrimination against you.

Similarly, in the employment context, it is indirect discrimination against married persons if the condition imposed is such that the proportion of married persons who can comply with it is considerably smaller than the proportion of single persons who can comply with it.

The following is an example of indirect discrimination. A woman, aged 35, applies for a particular post for which she has all the necessary qualifications. She is told by the employer that she cannot be considered for the post because they are looking for someone under the age of thirty. As many women between the mid-twenties and the mid-thirties are engaged in bearing and minding children, the condition that an applicant must be under thirty is such that the proportion of women who can comply with it is considerably smaller than the proportion of men who can comply with it. Unless the condition can be shown by the employer to be justifiable, it is indirect sex discrimination.

The question is not whether it is *theoretically* possible for women to comply with a condition, but whether they can do so *in practice*, bearing in mind current usual behaviour. In the above example it is, of course, possible in theory for women to comply with the condition. They don't have to get married, or to have children or to mind the children. They may find someone else to look after them, or as a last resort may put them into care. The practical position, however, is that many women between the mid-twenties and the mid-thirties are engaged in bearing and minding children, and most of them find it impossible to take up employment until they are in their thirties and the children have grown up.

You can only complain of indirect discrimination if you are adversely affected because you cannot comply with the discriminatory condition. In the above example, a 28-year-old woman who applied for the job could not complain of discrimination because the condition did not operate to her detriment. It may, however, be open to the Equal Opportunities Commission to take proceedings in respect of it (see page 137).

It is irrelevant that a woman could have complied with the necessary condition some time in the past. The relevant time for judging a woman's ability to comply with a requirement or condition is the date on which it is being applied to her to her detriment.

The fact that the condition or requirement imposed is such that *no woman* can comply with it is also irrelevant. For instance, a working men's club has a rule that only employees who are members are entitled to a disciplinary hearing. Women cannot be members of the club. A female employee is suspended without a disciplinary hearing. This would be indirect discrimination even though no woman could have complied with the requirement of being a member of the club.

What is meant by a 'requirement' or 'condition'?

The words 'requirement' and 'condition' do not have any special legal meaning, and are construed by the courts in accordance with their ordinary meaning.

It is, however, very important when you bring a case to court to clearly formulate the condition or requirement which you allege is discriminatory. It is not always easy to do this as requirements and conditions are often not made explicit, and you may have to examine carefully the practices and procedures before you can formulate a requirement or condition which adversely affects women. For example, a company employs full-time and part-time employees; all the part-time employees are women. A redundancy situation arises. The company's procedure is that the criterion 'last in first out' applies, save that the part-time workers are dismissed first. In this case, the employers had applied a requirement or condition that in order to rank in selection for redundancy by virtue of service and the principle of last in first out, the applicant had to be employed full-time.

Once you have defined a requirement or condition, you then have to show that it is a 'must' – something with which you have to comply in order to achieve what you want. It must be such that your failure to comply with it would mean that you could never get whatever it was that you wanted. It is not enough if the requirement or condition which you have formulated is one of many factors taken into account which make it more difficult to get what you want.

When is a discriminatory condition justifiable?

Once you have established that a condition exists, that the proportion of women (or married persons) who can comply with it is considerably smaller than the proportion of men (or single persons) who can comply with it, and that it is detrimental to you, then it is for the person imposing the condition to show that it is justifiable, notwithstanding its obvious discriminatory effect.

In order to show that a condition is justifiable, the person imposing it would have to prove that the measures chosen:

(a) correspond to a real need on the part of the undertaking,

(b) are appropriate with a view to achieving the objectives pursued and

(c) are necessary to that end.

Whether a discriminatory condition can be proved to be justifiable in accordance with the test set out above will depend on the facts of your individual case. The courts and tribunals will weigh the needs of the enterprise against the discriminatory effect of the condition, and will consider whether the person imposing the condition could achieve his object by some other non-discriminatory method.

Can the less favourable treatment of a pregnant woman amount to sex discrimination?

Yes. It is wrong to argue that it cannot be sex discrimination because there are no men in a similar position with whom a pregnant woman can compare herself.

The reason for a pregnant woman being treated less favourably is more often the consequences of the pregnancy rather than the condition itself. Thus a pregnant woman is usually treated less favourably, not because she is going to have a baby, but because of her enforced period of absence from work as a result of being pregnant.

The correct approach, therefore, is to compare the treatment of the pregnant woman with that of a male colleague who has to be absent from work for an equivalent period.

For example, a woman tells her employers that she is pregnant and that this will necessitate her being absent from work for six months. She is instantly dismissed. A male colleague had in the past been absent from work for five months because of an illness. The dismissal of the pregnant woman would amount to sex discrimination.

If a woman is dismissed because of pregnancy and has been in that employment for more than two years, she can bring a claim for unfair dismissal.

What if I am treated less favourably because I have young children?

If you are treated less favourably because you are a *woman* with young children, this may amount to direct discrimination against you on the basis of your sex. If someone treats both men and women with young children less favourably, this may amount to indirect discrimination against married persons.

For instance, a woman with three young children works as a waitress at a bistro. When the employer finds out that she has young children, he dismisses her. If he claimed that he had dismissed her because in his experience he had found *women* with young children to be unreliable employees, then it would be direct discrimination against the woman (because the employer would be treating her less favourably than men with young children). If, however, he claimed that he did not employ either men or women with young children because in his experience they were unreliable employees, then his conduct would amount to indirect discrimination against married persons, because a smaller proportion of married persons could comply with the 'no children' requirement than unmarried persons.

In general, a condition which excludes *all* members of a class from employment cannot be justified on the ground that some members of that class are unreliable employees. An employer must investigate each case and not simply apply a rule of convenience, or a prejudice, to exclude a whole class of women or married persons because some members of that class are not reliable employees.

In the above example the employer should not have applied a blanket rule excluding all women (or persons) with young children. He should have ascertained whether this particular employee was reliable or not. He could have done this by examining her past work record or by making inquiries as to what arrangements had been made to look after the children while she was at work.

What if I am treated less favourably because I am about to be married?

If a woman is treated unfavourably after announcing her intention to get married, it may be direct discrimination on the grounds of her sex. It would not amount to discrimination against married persons, because she would be a single person at the time the unfavourable treatment took place.

For instance, a woman is dismissed after her employers are told that she intends to get married. A man in a similar position would not be dismissed. This is direct discrimination against the woman. The same would apply if a woman is dismissed after announcing her intention to marry another employee in the same company, and the employers contend that it is against company policy to employ married couples.

Are the motives and intentions of the discriminator a relevant consideration?

The correct approach is to look at the factual nature of the act itself. The question to ask is – has there been less favourable treatment and is the reason for it the sex or the marital status of the individual concerned?

It is entirely irrelevant whether the discriminator intended or meant to discriminate. Thus it is no defence that the discriminator honestly believed the discrimination to be in the best interests of the victim.

For example, X, a woman, applies for a job on a painting and decorating team. She and another woman are due to start on a certain date. The other woman does not report for work. The personnel officer decides not to accept X because, as the other woman has not reported, she will be the only woman on the team. Problems had arisen in the past when there had been only one woman in the team. This is direct discrimination against X on the grounds of her sex. It is no defence for the employers to say that their decision had been taken with the best motives and in the interests of X, who might be subjected to a certain amount of harassment as the only woman on the team.

The same applies if a person imposes a condition or requirement without intending to discriminate against women, but the effect of that is discriminatory. Intention, however, is relevant in cases of indirect discrimination to the extent that no damages will be awarded if there was no intention to discriminate (see pages 84 and 124).

What if my sex is not the only reason for my being treated less favourably?

A person's conduct may still amount to sex discrimination even though your sex is not the *only* ground on which you are being treated less favourably.

However, in order to succeed in a claim for sex discrimination you would have to prove that the fact that you are a woman was a 'substantial' and 'effective' cause for the action which the person took. In other words, it was the major reason which prompted the action, and not just an incidental factor.

For example, Ms M works as a porter in a college, and the employers refuse to let her have the master key. A male porter is allowed to have it. If the main reason why they do not let her have it is that she lost it on a previous occasion when she was on duty, it is not sex discrimination. If, however, another female porter is not allowed to have the key, and the reason for it is that the employers regard all women as unreliable because of what happened with Ms M in the past, that would be sex discrimination.

Another example might be where a woman applies for a job in a warehouse. The work involves carrying and transporting heavy packages. If she is refused the job because the employers assume that as a woman she will not be able to carry the packages, then it is sex discrimination. If, however, she is given a trial and cannot carry the packages, then she is refused the job on the grounds of her physique and strength, and it is not sex discrimination.

It is important to remember that if you are a black woman, it may be that you are being discriminated against not only on the grounds of your sex, but also on racial grounds. In such a situation you are entitled to bring a claim for *both* sex *and* race discrimination. (For the law on race discrimination see *The Race Discrimination Handbook* in this series.)

Taking proceedings for sex discrimination does not prevent you from taking other proceedings. It may often be appropriate to bring one action alleging various forms of unlawful conduct. For instance, if you have been employed for more than two years, and are dismissed in circumstances that amount to sex discrimination, you may also be entitled to bring proceedings for unfair dismissal.

What if I am victimized for being involved in discrimination proceedings?

You can bring proceedings for discrimination against anyone who treats you less favourably than others in the same circumstances are treated or would be treated, and the reason for the less favourable treatment is one or more of the following:

(a) you have brought proceedings against that person or someone else under the Sex Discrimination Act 1975 (that is, for discrimination as defined above) or the Equal Pay Act 1970 (see pages 16–34);

(b) you have given evidence or information in connection with any proceedings brought under the Sex Discrimination Act 1975 or the Equal Pay Act 1970. (It does not matter if the information was given before any proceedings were actually begun so long as the victimization occurred at a time when proceedings had actually been brought, and the reason for it was the giving of the information.);

(c) you have done something 'by reference to' the Sex Discrimination Act 1975 or the Equal Pay Act 1970. This would cover, for example, the making of a report to the Equal Opportunities Commission that facts are available which ought to be investigated and which indicate a possible breach of either of the two Acts;

(d) you have alleged that someone has done something which would be an infringement of either the Sex Discrimination Act 1975 or the Equal Pay Act 1970. It is irrelevant that you do not specifically allege a breach of either of the two Acts, as long as the facts contained in your allegation amount to such an infringement;

(c) the person treating you less favourably knows that you intend to do one or more of the above things (a–d), or suspects that you have done or intend to do one or more of them.

If, however, you are being treated less favourably because of an allegation made by you, and your allegation is in fact false *and* was not made by you in good faith, then you cannot complain that you have been discriminated against by way of victimization.

Is every act of discrimination unlawful?

No. The Sex Discrimination Act 1975 specifies particular types of behaviour in certain fields which amount to unlawful discrimination. Thus, once you have established that you have been discriminated against on the grounds of your sex, marital status (in the employment field), or by way of victimization, the next question is whether the discrimination is unlawful.

Certain discriminatory conduct in relation to employment (see chapters 3 and 4), education (see chapter 6), housing and other premises (see chapter 7) and the provision of goods, facilities and services (see chapter 8) is unlawful discrimination.

In addition, the Equal Pay Act 1970 gives women employees certain rights. Basically a woman employee should be paid the same as a man when she is doing the same or broadly similar work, or when her work has been given the same value as his by a job evaluation scheme, or when she is doing work that is of equal value to a man's work. In addition to equal pay, any other terms and conditions of employment which are contained in her contract should be equal (see chapter 2).

It is important to realize that the law can only provide remedies for acts of unlawful discrimination or breaches of the Equal Pay Act 1970. It cannot in any way deal with sexist beliefs and attitudes. Thus sexism is not against the law; the law can only intervene and assist you if that sexism is translated into some kind of unlawful discriminatory act.

2: European Community Law and the Equal Pay Act 1970

What rights does the Equal Pay Act 1970 give?
The Equal Pay Act (hereinafter referred to as 'the EPA') was passed in 1970 but did not come into force until 1975. It gives identical rights to men and women but, as it is usually women workers who are treated less favourably in this respect, this chapter will deal with the topic on the basis of the rights conferred upon women workers. Any reference, therefore, to the rights of women workers applies equally to male workers.

The EPA gives women workers a right to equal terms and conditions of employment as a male worker where:

(a) the woman is employed on 'like work' with the male worker (for the meaning of 'like work', see page 22), or

(b) the woman does work which has been rated as equivalent to that of a male worker under a job evaluation study (see page 24), or

(c) the woman's work is of 'equal value' with that of the male worker (see page 27),

unless the employer can prove that the difference in the terms and conditions is genuinely due to a material factor other than the difference in sex (see page 29).

It is important to remember that the EPA applies not only to your basic wage or salary, but also to other aspects of remuneration contained in your contract. For instance, you are entitled to claim equality in respect of bonuses, sick pay, shift pay, overtime rates, free meals and any other payments in cash or in kind for work done by you. If there are other terms in your contract, not related to payment, which are less favourable than those of a male colleague, you should complain of sex discrimination (see chapter 3).

A woman is entitled to claim equality in respect of *any* term in her contract which is less favourable than that of a male colleague, even if her contract, looked at as a whole, is as favourable as that of the man. For instance, a woman's basic pay and overtime rates are less than that of a male colleague who is employed on like work with her. The woman, however, is provided with free meals, has an additional two days' paid holiday each year and enjoys better sickness pay benefits. The woman claims that she is entitled to the same basic pay and overtime rates as her male colleague. The correct approach in such a case is not to compare their respective 'pay packages' as a whole, to see if there is any difference, but to compare the particular terms in respect of which a complaint has been made.

Who is entitled to the rights under the EPA?
The right to claim equal pay without discrimination on grounds of sex is available to any person employed under a contract of service or of apprenticeship or a contract personally to execute any work or labour (for the meaning of these terms, see page 35).

The right is also available to employees of the Crown and government departments, with the exception of those in the armed forces and the holders of statutory office (for the exceptions, see below).

Are there any exclusions from the EPA?
Yes, there are certain provisions and categories of persons excluded from the protection given by the EPA. They are:

(a) provisions relating to retirement and pensions, except for terms or provisions which, in relation to retirement, afford access to opportunities for promotion, transfer or training or provide for a woman's dismissal or demotion. The effect of this is that it is lawful under the EPA for there to be a differential between men and women as to the age at which they become entitled to State pension (65 for men and 60 for women). It is, however, unlawful for an employer to provide for differential compulsory retirement ages for men and women in comparable positions;

(b) overseas employees, that is those who work wholly or mainly outside Great Britain (for further explanation of this, see page 37);

(c) terms affording special treatment to women in connection with pregnancy or childbirth;

(d) women in the armed forces. The EPA, however, states that the Secretary of State shall not make a distinction between men and women as regards pay, allowances or leave unless they are due to differences between the obligations undertaken by men and women;

(e) holders of statutory office. A statutory office is one that is created by an Act of Parliament. Lay magistrates and adjudicators who hear immigration appeals are examples of holders of statutory offices.

Does the EEC law make any provision for equal pay?

The Treaty of Rome was one of three treaties setting up the EEC. Article 119 of the Treaty lays down the principle that 'men and women should receive equal pay for equal work'. It defines 'pay' as 'the ordinary basic or minimum wage or salary and any other consideration, whether in cash or in kind, which the worker receives, directly or indirectly, in respect of his employment from his employer'.

In addition, there are two Directives which are relevant, the Equal Pay Directive and the Equal Treatment Directive.

The Equal Pay Directive explains the principle of equal pay, as set out in Article 119, as meaning 'for the same work or for work to which equal value is attributed, the elimination of all discrimination on grounds of sex with regard to all aspects and conditions of remuneration'. This Directive essentially explains how Article 119 ought to be applied in practice, and does not in any way alter or add anything to the principle contained in that Article.

The Equal Treatment Directive lays down the principle of equal treatment of men and women as regards access to employment, training, working conditions, promotion and dismissal. It states that there should be no discrimination whatsoever on the grounds of sex, either directly or indirectly, nor by reference to marital or family status. There are three exceptions whereby discrimination is permitted. These are discrimination where being of a particular sex is a genuine occupational qualification (see pages 40–3), discrimination in favour of women in relation to pregnancy and maternity, and measures to promote equal opportunity and remove existing inequalities which affect women's opportunities in access to employment, promotion, training and working conditions.

Does the EEC law apply in UK courts and tribunals?

Article 119 of the Treaty of Rome (see above) applies to all cases where a direct comparison can be made between men and women doing like work, equivalently rated work or work of equal value, but receiving different pay in respect of it. Where Article 119 applies directly to the facts of the case, it is binding on the English courts and tribunals, and the individual has a right to rely on it in a claim for equal pay in the English courts and tribunals.

When you bring a claim for equal pay, it is always worth relying on Article 119 as well as the law of this country, that is the EPA. This is because Article 119 is wider in scope and applies to certain situations to which the EPA does not apply (for example, see page 21).

The position with the two EEC Directives (see pages 18–19) is slightly different. You can rely on a Directive in an English court or tribunal if your claim for equal pay is against a State authority. Employees in the private sector cannot rely on them in their claims for equal pay. It is up to the courts to decide what is a State authority. Area Health Authorities and Chief Constables are examples of what constitute a State authority. It is, however, open to a private sector employee relying on Article 119 to use the wording of the Equal Pay Directive to expand upon and explain the principle stated in Article 119.

With whom must I compare myself?

It is absolutely essential for a claim under the EPA that there be a man with whom you can compare yourself. If there is no such man, then you have no chance of success under the EPA.

You must compare yourself with a man who is:

(a) working for the same employer as you or for 'an associated employer'. Two employers are treated as 'associated' either if one is a company of which the other (directly or indirectly) has control or if both are companies of which a third person (directly or indirectly) has control; *and*

(b) working either at the same establishment as you, or at establishments in Great Britain which include the one at which you are working *and* at which there are common terms and conditions of employment either for employees generally or for employees of the relevant classes.

It is for you to select the man with whom you want to compare yourself, and not for the tribunal. The tribunal is not entitled to substitute the person you have selected with one of their choice.

You are not restricted to choosing only one man with whom to compare yourself; you are perfectly entitled to compare yourself with as many men as you like. Obviously the larger the number of men you compare yourself with, the greater the likelihood of you being awarded equal pay with at least one of them.

If you work in a large organization, it may be difficult for you to select a man with whom to compare yourself as you may not have precise information about the work being done by other employees. In such a case, as long as you have a *prima facie* case (that is, some basis for making your claim), you can ask the tribunal to order your employers to make available to you such documents as the job descriptions of the other employees.

It is not essential that you compare yourself with a man who is *at present* doing the same kind of work as you, as long as there was a man recently employed on such work. Under the EPA, you should, however, be able to point to a particular time when both of you were doing the same kind of work. The effect of the EPA would then be to insert a clause into your contract, raising your pay to the same level as his. If he then moves on to do a different kind of work, or leaves the job, your pay should remain at the raised level. For example, waitresses at a hotel are paid £1.30 an hour. The hotel then employs a waiter who is paid £1.50 an hour. After two weeks of working as a waiter he is promoted to banqueting supervisor. The waitresses are entitled to compare themselves with him and claim £1.50 an hour, not only for the two weeks during which he worked as a waiter, but thereafter until something else happens to alter their contracts.

As has been stated above, under the EPA it is necessary to show that you and the man with whom you are comparing yourself were at some stage *contemporaneously* (i.e. at the same time) doing the same kind of work. Therefore, under the EPA, you cannot compare yourself with a man who was employed either prior to or subsequent to your period of employment.

There is no such restriction under Article 119 of the

Treaty of Rome which is directly applicable and enforceable in English courts and tribunals (see page 19). Therefore, if you discover that a male predecessor, who was doing the same kind of work as you, was being paid more than you are, you can claim equal pay in the tribunal under Article 119. You can also claim equal pay with a male successor in the same circumstances, provided that six months have not lapsed since you left the employment in question. It would then be a question of fact for the tribunal to decide whether the difference in pay between two workers occupying the same posts, but at different periods of time, may be explained by the operation of factors which are unconnected with any discrimination on the grounds of sex.

Article 119 does not, however, entitle you to claim a higher salary on the basis that, had you been a man, you would have been paid a better salary. There must be a man who is either currently performing, or has previously or subsequently performed similar work.

What is meant by employed on 'like work'?

You are employed on like work with a man if:

(a) your work and his are of the same or a broadly similar nature, and

(b) there is no difference, or no important difference, between the tasks that you and he actually perform.

The correct approach is to consider these two aspects separately. First, the tribunal must decide whether your work and his are of the same or a broadly similar nature. In so doing, it should consider the matter in broad general terms, and should assess the similarity of the *nature* of the work. It should not at this stage analyse in detail the tasks performed by the two workers. The test is the similarity of what is done, and the similarity of the skill and knowledge required to do it.

If the tribunal concludes that the work is of the same or

a broadly similar nature, it must then go on to consider the differences between what you do and what the man does. If there are any differences, the tribunal should have regard to the frequency with which these differences occur in practice, as well as to the nature and extent of the differences.

The important thing to remember is that a difference in contractual obligations is not in itself sufficient to say that there are differences between what you and the man do. The tribunal will approach it by looking at what happens *in practice*, and see if there are any differences between what you and the man *actually* do, as opposed to differences in what you and he *may be required* to do. For example, a factory employs men and women to work on their production line. Both men and women work on the same track and perform identical tasks. The men, however, are paid a higher basic rate than the women. The employers contend that this is because the men have additional contractual obligations, such as working compulsory overtime and working at night. The tribunal would look at what happens in practice. If the men had, in fact, never been asked to work overtime or at nights, then in reality there would be no difference between what the men and the women did. Even if the men did sometimes work overtime or night shifts, the tribunal would look at how frequently they did so and the tasks they performed when they did. If the tasks were exactly the same as when they worked alongside with the women during the day, and required no extra skill or ability, the employer could not justify paying them a higher basic rate. The employer is, of course, entitled to pay them an additional premium for working nights and overtime.

If there are any differences between what you and the man do, the tribunal will consider the frequency with which these differences occur. For example, a man and a woman both work as clerk-typists in the same department.

The man is also a trainee manager, and as such his contract stipulates that he may from time to time be required to do the job of a transport supervisor. In the four years that he has been employed by the company, he has only done the job of a transport supervisor for a total period of five weeks. The difference between what the man and the woman did would not be an important difference because it is something which happened so infrequently.

It may be an important difference between what a man and a woman do if one has a far greater degree of responsibility than the other. This would apply, for instance, where an error by the one would have far more serious consequences than an error by the other. For example, a man and a woman work in the same department in a factory and both are responsible for ordering materials. The materials that the woman orders are never worth more than £2.50 each. The materials that the man orders are usually worth £500–£1,000 each. It would be an important factor to take into account that an error by the man would have more serious consequences than an error by the woman.

What is meant by 'work rated as equivalent'?

A woman is employed on work rated as equivalent with that of a man if their jobs have been given equal value by a job evaluation study. The purpose of a job evaluation study (JES) is to grade the jobs done by various employees in terms of the demand made on a worker under various headings (for instance, effort, skill, responsibility). One is concerned here primarily with the value given to a particular job, and not with the skills or qualifications of the individual.

There is no strict formula laid down as to how a job evaluation study ought to be carried out. The following are the most commonly used methods of evaluating jobs:

Job Ranking
Each job is looked at as a whole and is given a ranking in relation to all other jobs. A table is then drawn up listing the jobs according to their rank, and the list is divided into grades.

Paired Comparisons
Each job is compared as a whole with each other job in turn, and is awarded points according to whether its importance is more or less than, or equal to that other job. The points awarded in each comparison are then added up, and the job is ranked on the basis of its total score.

Job Classification
This involves drawing up a grading structure first, and fitting each job into the structure.

Points Assessment
This is the most common system in use. This method breaks down each job into a number of factors, such as skill, responsibility, physical and mental requirements and working conditions. A scale is determined whereby each factor carries a certain number of points. Certain factors may be weighted, in that more points will attach to them. Each factor in a job is then awarded points according to the predetermined scale, and the total points decide a job's place in the ranking order.

A job evaluation study may be carried out by the employers themselves, or by outside consultants commissioned by them. It will normally involve consultation and negotiation with your union. If such a study is about to be carried out at your place of work, make sure that you and/or your union are involved from the start. Find out which formula is to be used, how the points are to be awarded, and if you feel that this in any way discriminates against women, challenge it before the scheme is actually introduced. If you already have a discriminatory scheme, get your trade union to renegotiate it.

No matter what form the JES takes it is, subject to two exceptions, conclusive evidence as to whether a woman's job is or is not of the same value as that of a man. Thus, if your job has been given a lower grading than that of a man, you cannot succeed in your claim for equal pay, unless you can prove that you and the man are doing like work (see page 22). However, faced with an adverse JES, it will be extremely unlikely that you will succeed under that head. If, however, your job has been given the same value as that of a male colleague, then your claim will succeed unless the employer can show that the difference in pay is genuinely due to a material factor other than the difference in sex (see page 29).

The two situations in which a JES will not be conclusive evidence as to the values given to particular jobs are as follows:

(a) where it is left to the employer to determine which grade a particular employee fits into according to the *employer's* evaluation of that *employee's work.* In such a case the JES would not be valid. In order for it to be so, it should be possible by applying the study to determine the position of a particular employee at a particular point in a particular salary grade without taking other matters into account.

It is, nevertheless, open to an employer to pay one employee more than another in the same grade on the basis of some personal attribute of that employee, such as seniority or better qualifications.

(b) where sex discrimination is built into the scheme itself. This would apply, for instance, where the factors which were used to evaluate the jobs were those that were more relevant to the men's job than to the women's job, or where more points were awarded to criteria for which male employees showed a particular aptitude. For instance, a company employs women to manufacture children's toys. The women work in cramped conditions in a basement. The firm employs men to transport the finished product. Their job involves loading the lorries, driving them to their destination and then unloading them. The job evaluation study would be discriminatory and, therefore, invalid if either it took into account only criteria which were relevant to the men's job, such as muscular effort, physical strength required, driving skills, and ignored those which were relevant to the women's job, such as manual dexterity, working conditions, or if it awarded higher points to the former.

What is meant by 'work of equal value'?

In order to make an 'equal value' claim, a woman has to show that she is employed on work which is in terms of the demands made on her (for instance, under such headings as effort, skill and decision) of equal value to that of a man in the same employment. The effect of this is that a woman can compare herself with a man doing a completely different job, and can succeed in her claim if she can show that, regardless of their different titles, her job is just as demanding as his.

If the man with whom the woman is comparing herself is doing 'like work' (see page 22) or 'equivalently rated work' (see page 24), then she must bring her claim under whichever of those two headings applies, and cannot make an equal value claim. There is nothing to stop her making an equal value claim just because there is some other man who is employed on like or equivalently rated work. For example, a woman makes a claim for equal pay with X, a male worker who is doing different work, on the basis that her work is of equal value to his. She is not in any way stopped from making that claim simply because there is another male worker, Y, who is doing like or equivalently rated work, and being paid the same as her.

There is a special and complicated procedure which relates to an equal value claim. Once an equal value claim has been raised, the tribunal holds a preliminary hearing to decide whether it should refer the matter to an independent expert. It will *not* refer the matter to an independent expert if any of the following three conditions apply:

(a) the tribunal takes the view that the woman's case is hopeless, and that it would be a waste of time and money to refer it to an expert;

(b) there has already been a job evaluation study which has rated the man's and the woman's work differently, unless it can be shown that the job evaluation study was itself discriminatory (see page 26); or

(c) the employer proves that the difference in pay is genuinely due to a material factor other than the difference of sex (see page 29). This is a 'defence' to an equal value claim, but there is nothing to prevent the employer from raising it at the preliminary hearing.

If none of the above conditions apply, the tribunal *must* refer the matter to an independent expert, and adjourn the hearing until a report is prepared by the expert. The expert is chosen from a panel drawn up by ACAS (Advisory, Conciliation and Arbitration Service). The expert is normally expected to produce a report within six weeks, although in reality it often takes much longer. Both parties may make representations to the expert, and he or she may seek and acquire whatever other information is thought necessary. A draft copy of the report will then be sent to both parties, who will be invited to make their comments on it. The final report should include a summary of the representations made by the parties.

Once the tribunal receives the report, it will send copies to both parties and notify them of the date when the hearing will resume. Unless the tribunal feels that the report is unsatisfactory (for instance, because the expert did not follow the correct procedure, or because no reasonable expert could have reached that particular conclusion on the available evidence), it will become part of the evidence. Either party can ask for the expert to attend the hearing, for the purpose of cross-examination. There is nothing to stop the woman making the claim from commissioning her own report and calling her own expert evidence at the hearing. Having heard all the evidence, the tribunal will then decide whether the woman's work is or is not of equal value to that of the man.

Am I entitled to equal pay once I have established one of the above three?

Once you have proved that you are employed on like work, equivalently rated work, or work of equal value with that of a male colleague, you are entitled to the same pay as him, *unless* the employer can prove either:

(a) (this applies in all three cases) that the difference in pay was due to a genuine material difference, other than the difference of sex, between your case and his; or

(b) (this applies only to an equal value claim) that there was some other material factor, other than the difference of sex, which justified the differential in pay.

Both these defences are explained in greater detail below.

What material differences, apart from sex, might affect my entitlement to equal pay?

The employer has to prove, first, that there is a material difference between the woman's case and the man's case, and secondly, that the difference in pay is genuinely due to that material difference.

Obviously the difference must be an important and significant difference, and not just a slight or trivial one.

Nor indeed must it be a difference between the tasks carried out by the man and the woman, because that will already have been examined when determining whether or not they are employed on like work. The following are examples of what may amount to a material difference: greater length of service, more experience, better qualifications, greater skill, higher productivity, considerations of merit such as time-keeping, efficiency, reliability, etc., geographical location of the workplace (i.e. London weighting), paying in accordance with nationally, or widely negotiated salary scales.

The position until recently was that in order to see whether there was a material difference, one simply looked at the 'personal equation', that is his circumstances and her circumstances, and one did not take into account any outside factors. That is not the position any more. An employer can now rely on the 'material difference defence' if he can prove that there are objectively justified grounds for the pay differential. These grounds may be economic factors which affect the efficient carrying on of the employer's business, or administrative efficiency in a concern not engaged in commerce or business. In order to prove that the differential in pay is objectively justified on economic grounds, the employer would have to prove that the measures chosen by him correspond to a real need on the part of the undertaking, are appropriate with a view to achieving the objectives pursued and are necessary to that end.

For example, all the part-time employees in a company are women, and all the full-time employees are men. The women are employed on like work with the men. The men are paid a higher hourly rate than the women. The employer cannot justify the pay differential on the basis that there is a material difference, namely that the women are part-time employees and the men are full-time employees. If the employer intended to discriminate against women by paying part-time workers less, then he has no defence. Even if there was no such intention, in order to succeed the employer must show that the difference in pay between full-time and part-time workers is necessary in order to obtain some result (other than cheap female labour) which the employer desires for economic or other reasons.

Once a material difference has been established, the next question is whether the difference in pay is *genuinely* due to that difference, or is what is taking place simply a hidden form of sex discrimination? For example, the owners of a chain of betting shops employ two female counterhands in all their shops, except in a small number of shops which are located in awkward and difficult areas where they believe that there might be trouble. In these shops, they employ one male counterhand and one female. The male counterhand is paid more than the female. The employers contend that the difference in pay is due to a material difference, which is that the man is there to play a protective role in case of trouble. In such a case, the employers would lose because what they are doing is simply paying the man more because he is a man, not because he had some special training in martial arts, or previous experience as a security guard. The difference in pay is not *genuinely* due to a material difference other than the difference of sex.

Two types of material difference deserve a special mention. These are differential grades and 'red ringing'.

Differential grades

The fact that a man and a woman are on different grades or on different salary scales may be a genuine material difference justifying a difference in pay. This, however, is based on the assumption that the manner in which the grades and salary scales were determined was not in itself discriminatory on the grounds of sex. For example, a man and a woman are employed by a local authority and doing like work. They are employed under different nationally negotiated salary scales. Both scales comprise both men and women. The result is that the man is paid more than the woman. In such a case, a material difference defence would probably succeed. If, however, one grade or scale consists entirely or predominantly of men, and the other of women, then the defence would probably fail because it would appear that the grading itself was on the basis of sex.

'Red ringing'

'Red ringing' or 'red circling' takes place when an employer moves higher graded employees to a lower grade, but nevertheless maintains their higher rate of pay. An example of this would be where X, a man, is employed on a Grade 1 job. The Grade 1 position then becomes redundant and X is moved to the lower Grade 2 job, but continues to receive the higher Grade 1 salary. The effect of this is to protect his personal wage and thus bring him within what is known as the 'red circle'.

The question that then arises is whether Y, a woman, who is either currently employed on or subsequently recruited on a Grade 2 job, can claim that she is entitled to the same pay as X. The answer to this depends on all the facts of the case. If both men and women had been employed on the original Grade 1, and therefore there were both men and women within the 'red circle', then Y would probably fail in her claim for equal pay with X. The reason for this would be that the employer could show that the difference in their salaries was due to a genuine material difference other than sex.

If, however, the original grading system itself had been based on sex discrimination, then Y would probably succeed in her claim. This would apply, for instance, where the grading structure had been such that it had been impossible for women ever to enter into Grade 1. Where the 'red circle' consists only of men, this must raise a suspicion as to whether the initial grading was itself discriminatory.

Material factor

As stated above, in an equal value claim the employer can justify the differential in pay not only by relying on a genuine material difference between the woman's case and the man, but can in addition justify it on the basis of some other material factor. The effect of this is to enable a tribunal to take into account market forces and economic factors in deciding whether a woman should be paid the same as a man whose work is of equal value to hers.

In order successfully to rely on this defence, an employer must prove that:

(a) the factor being relied upon is *material*, in the sense that it is significant and relevant, and not unimportant and trivial;

(b) the factor is not the difference in sex;

(c) there are objectively justified grounds for paying the woman less, that is, that the measures chosen by the employer correspond to a *real need* on the part of the undertaking, are appropriate with a view to achieving the objectives pursued and are *necessary* to that end; and

(d) the pay differential is *genuinely* due to that material factor.

How do I make a claim for equal pay?

You make an application to the industrial tribunal (for procedure in the industrial tribunal, see chapter 5).

What do I get if I am successful?

If you are successful the relevant terms of your contract will be automatically changed to be the same as the man's with whom you were comparing yourself. You can be given back-pay, that is, the difference between what you were paid and what you ought to have been paid, for up to a period of two years before the date on which you made your complaint.

3: Discrimination by Employers

Who is an employer?

For the purposes of sex discrimination, an employer is someone who hires people to work for him or her either under a contract of service or apprenticeship or under a contract personally to execute any work or labour.

Before you can claim that someone is your employer, it is essential for you to show that there is a contract of some sort between you and that person. A contract is a legally binding agreement between two persons, whereby each agrees to do something for the other. In the context of a job, the agreement would normally be a promise by you to do work for the employer in return for his promise to pay you wages for it. If you do not have a contractual relationship with the individual concerned, then that person is not your employer.

Being hired under 'a contract of service' simply means that you are working for the persons concerned as their employee, as opposed to doing work for them in your capacity as a self-employed person. The question of whether you are an employee or a self-employed person will depend on all the circumstances of your working relationship. The presence of the following factors would tend to show that you are an employee: a certain degree of control over how and when you do your work; a fixed remuneration paid at regular intervals; the fact that you are tied to one employer and are not free to work for others; the fact that income tax and national insurance contributions are paid on your behalf by the person for whom you work; and the fact that the working relationship can be terminated by dismissal by the person for whom you are working. In order to determine this question all aspects of the relationship have to be considered, as no single factor is in itself decisive.

A 'contract personally to execute any work or labour' is a wide and flexible term and may in some situations include self-employed persons. In order to determine whether you are employed under such a contract, two questions have to be answered. First, whether your duties constitute work or labour, and, second, the extent to which you are required to execute the duties yourself. You must be under an obligation to do some part of the work yourself, and not merely be responsible for seeing that the work is carried out. There is no strict rule as to the precise degree of personal involvement required in the execution of work to bring it within the definition. On the one hand, the smallest element of personal involvement will not necessarily bring a contract within the definition; on the other hand, you do not have to go so far as to show that all the work will be carried out by you personally. Whether your contract comes within the definition will depend on all the facts of your case.

For example, the Post Office refuses to appoint a woman as a sub-postmaster. A sub-postmaster has to undertake that certain things will be done – he or she would have to provide premises and ensure that services are provided by the Post Office to members of the public. There is, however, no obligation under the contract for the postmaster to do anything personally; all the work can be delegated. In such a case, the woman could not argue that the Post Office was her employer.

Against whom must an employer not discriminate?

It is unlawful for an employer to discriminate on the grounds of sex or marital status against those who work for him or her, those who are looking for work (this includes job applicants) and 'contract workers'.

You are a 'contract worker' if your case falls into the following category: you are employed by A, with whom you have a contract. A has a contract with B, another employer, to provide him with workers on a temporary basis. A sends you to work for B for a short time. You, of course, do not have any contract with B, so he is not your employer. It is, nevertheless, unlawful for B to discriminate against you on the basis of your sex or your marital status, and if he does so you can bring proceedings against him.

For example, you are a cleaner and you are employed by Cleaning Services Ltd, with whom you have a contract. Cleaning Services Ltd has a contract with a hotel to provide them with cleaners. You are sent temporarily to work at the hotel. If the hotel discriminates against you, you can bring proceedings against the hotel, although you have no contract with them and they are not your employers.

Can I complain of sex discrimination if the job is overseas?

No, you cannot. Sex discrimination is unlawful *only* in relation to employment at an establishment in Great Britain (that includes British territorial waters). If you do your work *wholly or mainly* outside Britain, then you are not employed at an establishment in this country, and you cannot complain of sex discrimination.

The position is slightly different if you work on board a ship registered at a port in Great Britain, or on an aircraft or hovercraft registered in the United Kingdom and operated by a person who has his principal place of business, or is ordinarily resident, in Great Britain. In such a case you will be treated as being employed at an establishment in Great Britain, unless you do your work *wholly* outside Britain.

What is unlawful discrimination when I am looking for a job?
It is unlawful for an employer to discriminate against you on the basis of your sex or your marital status in any of the following respects:

(a) The arrangements made by the employer for the purpose of determining who should be offered the job. 'Arrangements' is a wide term and includes the following: discriminatory advertising (see page 131); instructions to employment agencies, careers offices or a personnel department to discriminate (see page 134); recruitment procedures which have a discriminatory effect and, therefore, make it more difficult for women to get the jobs; appointing a person who is biased against women to conduct interviews, even though the employer did not know that the person was so biased; conducting interviews in a way which shows bias against women or women with children; excluding from the short-list on the basis of sex or marital status; imposing selection criteria, requirements or conditions which discriminate against women and/or married persons and are not justifiable, such as age limits (see page 6), not employing people who have young children (see page 9).

The following are examples of what may amount to discriminatory arrangements:

A large company interviews persons for the post of management trainees. The single women applicants are asked questions about whether they plan to get married and have a family. The single male applicants are not asked any questions about marriage or raising a family.

A woman applies for the post of professional at a golf course. She is not short-listed for the job, although she is better qualified than the three male applicants who are short-listed. At the interview she had been asked questions such as 'Are there any women golf professionals?' and 'Do you think men respond as well to a woman golf professional as to a man?'

The employer's behaviour remains unlawful even if in the event the post is not offered to anyone. The illegality lies in the making of the discriminatory arrangements.

(b) Not offering you the job. The refusal to offer you the job can occur in a variety of ways. You may be short-listed but not offered the job although your qualifications and experience make you a more suitable candidate than the man who is appointed; you may be invited for an interview but not short-listed although you are more qualified and experienced than the men who are; or you may not even be invited for an interview.

(c) The offer of a job on less favourable terms than those offered to a man or a single person. If you are being discriminated against as a woman (as opposed to as a married person), this only applies where the less favourable terms offered are one or more of the following:

(i) a non-contractual term;

(ii) a contractual term in respect of which you could successfully make a claim under the Equal Pay Act 1970 (see chapter 2) if you accepted the job;

(iii) a contractual term, not related to the payment of money, in respect of which you could not make a claim under the Equal Pay Act even if you accepted the job, because there is no man in the same employment with whom you could compare yourself (see page 20).

The following examples indicate how this works in practice:

An employer offers to pay you lower wages than are paid to existing male employees or to a male employee who is hired at the same time as you. If you accepted the job, would you be in a position to bring a successful claim under the Equal Pay Act 1970 (see chapter 2)? If the answer to that question is 'yes', then you can complain of unlawful sex discrimination in relation to the offer.

An employer offers you a post at a certain salary.

There are no male employees in the particular company. You know that the salary you are being offered is lower than that which is being paid to men holding the same post as you in other companies. You feel that your company would have offered you a higher salary had you been a man. The less favourable term which you are being offered is a contractual term related to the payment of money. You could, therefore, not complain of unlawful sex discrimination under (i) or (iii) above. Nor could you complain under (ii) because you would not succeed in a claim under the Equal Pay Act 1970, because there is no man with whom you could compare yourself. In such a case, therefore, you could not complain of unlawful sex discrimination.

If the term relates to payment of money, which is not part of your contract, you can complain of unlawful sex discrimination. For instance, an employer tells you at an interview that the company pays out discretionary bonuses at Christmas and that you can expect to receive about £200. A male applicant for the same post is told that he can expect to receive about £400. This would be unlawful sex discrimination in the offer of employment.

Is discrimination against prospective employees ever allowed?

Yes it is in the following circumstances:

Genuine occupational qualification

An employer can discriminate against women in the arrangements he makes for recruiting or by not offering women a job if it can be shown that being a man is a 'genuine occupational qualification' for the job. The same, of course, applies in reverse, that is, discrimination against men where being a woman is a 'genuine occupational qualification' for the job, and all references to 'a man' and 'a woman' in this part should be read and understood accordingly.

Being a man is a genuine occupational qualification for the job only if some or all of the duties of the job fall into one of the following categories:

(a) the essential nature of the job calls for a man for reasons of physiology (for example, male models) or authenticity in dramatic performances or other entertainment (for example, actors, singers and dancers). The word 'physiology' here is not referring to physical strength or stamina. Thus an employer acts unlawfully if arrangements are made to recruit men only simply because the job requires physical strength or stamina. The reason for that is that such arrangements would have been made on the assumption that women do not have strength or stamina;

(b) the job needs to be done by a man in order to preserve decency or privacy. There are two situations in which this may occur. First, the job is likely to involve physical contact with men in circumstances where they might reasonably object to it being carried out by a woman. This would apply, for instance, to security staff who have to frisk people, or to masseurs. Secondly, the woman is likely to do her work in circumstances where men might reasonably object to the presence of a woman because they are in a state of undress or using sanitary facilities. The obvious example is the job of a lavatory attendant;

(c) the job involves working or living in a private home where there could be reasonable objection to a woman doing the job because it would involve a degree of physical or social contact with a person living in the home, or knowledge of intimate details of such a person's life. Examples of this would be a nurse looking after a member of the family, or a close companion to an elderly member of the family. It would not, however, apply to a cook or a gardener in a large household;

(d) the nature or location of the job would make it impracticable for a female worker to live anywhere other than in the premises provided by the employer, and the only premises which are available are lived in, or normally lived in, by men, and there is no separate sleeping accommodation for women and no sanitary facilities which could be used by women in privacy. The exclusion of women from such a job is only lawful if the employer can show that it is not reasonable to expect him to provide the necessary facilities for women either in the same premises or elsewhere. This applies to jobs in remote places such as oil rigs, lighthouses and ships;

(e) the job involves working in a hospital, prison or some other place for people needing special care, supervision or attention (such as an old people's home, a probation hostel, a drugs rehabilitation centre, a mental home), and all the individuals in that particular establishment are men. In addition, an employer must show that it is reasonable, having regard to the essential character of the place in question, that the job should not be held by a woman. Thus, the mere fact that a particular institution is a single-sex institution is not in itself enough;

(f) the job is to provide people with personal welfare, education or other services, and those services can most effectively be provided by a man. This is a very vague phrase, and it is not entirely clear in which circumstances a service can be most effectively provided by a man. It could apply to probation officers, social workers and welfare workers. It could be said that a male probation officer would be best equipped to work with young men, on the basis that they might respond better to him than they would to a female probation officer. That appears, however, to be an unreliable generalization which does not take into account the abilities and experience of the individual probation officers and the personalities of the young men involved;

(g) the job needs to be held by a man because of restrictions imposed by the laws regulating the employment of women. This refers to the laws which used to exist allegedly to 'protect' women. However, most of these protective laws have now been repealed;

(h) the job has to be held by a man because it would involve working outside the UK in a country whose laws or customs are such that the work could not effectively be carried out by a woman. This might apply, for instance, to a sales representative who has to work in Saudi Arabia or Iran;

(i) the job is one of two to be held by a married couple. An example of this would be caretakers in an old people's home.

An employer is not allowed to discriminate against a potential female employee on any of the above grounds if at the time in question there were existing male employees who were capable of carrying out the relevant duties, whom it would have been reasonable to employ on those duties, and there were enough of them to carry out those duties without undue inconvenience.

Ministers of religion

A religious sect can refuse to employ female (or male) ministers if the doctrines of the religion so demand or if to do so would offend the religious susceptibilities of a significant number of its followers. Thus a Sikh temple is acting lawfully when it insists on employing only male priests.

Prison Officers

It is lawful to discriminate between male and female prison officers in requirements as to height.

Miners

An employer can discriminate against women by refusing

to employ them if the job normally involves spending a significant proportion of the time underground.

General exceptions
See chapter 10.

What is unlawful discrimination at my workplace?
It is unlawful for an employer to discriminate against you on the basis of your sex or marital status in any of the following ways:

(a) By restricting or denying you access to opportunities for promotion, transfer or training;

(b) By restricting or denying you access to other benefits, facilities or services;

(c) By dismissing you; or

(d) By subjecting you to any other detriment.

Each of these is looked at more closely below.

Promotion, transfer or training
The following are examples of what may amount to unlawful sex discrimination in relation to training and promotion:

Employees at a clerical level are graded 1 to 4. Grade 1 and 2 employees are predominantly women, Grade 3 and 4 predominantly men. The employers make arrangements for employees to attend training courses to learn to operate word processors. However, the training is only offered to employees at Grades 3 and 4, although those at 1 and 2 are perfectly capable of doing it, and would benefit from the training. This is indirect discrimination against the women employees.

Other examples may be where an employer makes arrangements for training courses to take place in the evenings or at weekends, times at which fewer women would be able to attend because of family commitments.

A woman has worked as an assistant manager for a

number of years and has often, in the absence of the manager, been asked to assume his duties and responsibilities. When the manager leaves, the post is advertised. The woman applies for promotion to the post of manager. An external male applicant, who is less qualified and experienced than her, is appointed to the post. Unless the employer could come forward with a very convincing concrete reason for appointing the man, this would be direct sex discrimination.

Sometimes discrimination in promotion may stem from earlier discrimination which existed at the workplace. For instance, a workplace has two types of full-time employees, permanent employees and temporary employees. Prior to 1975 (when the Sex Discrimination Act was passed) all the former were men and all the latter women. Promotion to a senior post is based on the length of experience as a permanent employee. As far as the women are concerned, their experience as permanent employees starts only from 1975. This would probably be indirect sex discrimination against a woman who applied to be promoted, but was disqualified because she did not have enough seniority in the relevant post.

There are, however, two exceptions when discrimination is allowed. First, your employer may discriminate against you by not offering you the opportunities for promotion, transfer or training for a particular post if being a man is a 'genuine occupational qualification' for that post (for the meaning of 'genuine occupational qualification' see page 40).

Secondly, an employer is allowed to a limited extent to discriminate positively. If at any time within the last twelve months there were either no women doing a particular job or the number of women doing it was comparatively small, an employer may discriminate positively by:

(a) providing training for the women employees only for that particular job; or

(b) encouraging women employees only to take advantage of opportunities for doing that particular job. This does not give an employer the right to appoint women only to the post in question. That would be unlawful sex discrimination against men. The employer is, however, entitled to encourage women only to apply for that post, or to encourage women only to undergo the relevant training for that post.

Benefits, facilities or other services

The first thing to remember is that this applies not only to the benefits, facilities and services which are provided by your employer, but also to those provided by others to which your employer has power to give you access. For instance, you work for a travel agency. The agency has an arrangement with certain hotels so that agency employees staying in the hotels get a 10% reduction. That is not a benefit provided directly by your employer, but it is in his power to decide whether or not you get that benefit. If you find that your male colleagues are being given the opportunity to take advantage of it, and you are not, then you can complain of sex discrimination.

Secondly, this provision does not apply to your wages or any payment of money which is regulated by your contract. If you are treated less favourably in that respect, you must complain under the Equal Pay Act provided, of course, that there is a man with whom you can compare yourself (see chapter 2). It applies to all matters that are not determined by your contract, and to things which are in your contract but are not related to the payment of money and are not covered by the Equal Pay Act. Thus you can complain of sex discrimination if you are not given a Christmas bonus whilst your male colleagues are, or if your male colleagues are given a larger expense allowance than you are, or if your male colleagues are given an opportunity to do overtime and you are not.

If your employer provides benefits, facilities or services to the general public, you must work out whether you have been discriminated against as a member of the public or as an employee. You will have been discriminated against as an employee if the benefits, etc. which the employer provides to the public are materially different from those which he provides to his employees, or if the provision of the relevant benefits, etc. is part of your contract of employment, or if the benefits, etc. relate to training. The following example indicates how this works in practice:

You work for a bank which has no special arrangement for giving loans to its employees. You apply for a loan to your bank. They ask you, as indeed they ask all female applicants for a loan, whether or not employed by them, to provide a male guarantor. This is unlawful sex discrimination, but you have been discriminated against as a member of the public and not as an employee. If, however, the bank gives its employees loans at a lower rate of interest, but is only prepared to give you a loan at the usual rate of interest, then it is discriminating against you as an employee.

The law, as it stands, seems to say that employers *can* discriminate in the provision of access to benefits, facilities and services, if they relate to retirement. It is, therefore, not entirely clear whether employers can discriminate in relation to their own pension schemes. English law seems to say that they can. EEC law makes a distinction between State pension schemes, which can lawfully discriminate between men and women, and employers' pension schemes, which probably cannot. Thus the fact that men and women become entitled to State pension at different ages (men at 65 and women at 60) is lawful. If, however, an employer differentiates between men and women as to the age at which they become entitled to a pension under the employer's scheme that would probably be unlawful.

It is not always clear when the provision of a particular benefit, etc. relates to retirement, and when it does not. For instance, British Rail employees, both male and female, get cheaper travel facilities for themselves and their families. Male employees continue to enjoy those facilities after retirement, but retired female employees get cheaper travel facilities only for themselves and not their families. There is no doubt that this is discrimination against the female employees in access to benefits. But the question is whether it is 'a provision in relation to retirement', because if it is then it is lawful and if it is not it is unlawful. The answer appears to be that it is not a provision in relation to retirement as it is merely the continuation of an existing benefit after retirement. The same would appear to apply to other privileges such as continued membership of a sporting or social club, the membership of which was restricted to employees, or the privilege of being allowed to continue to buy the employer's products at a favourable rate.

Finally, discrimination is allowed if the provision in question relates to death. For example, an employer has a pension scheme which provides for survivors' benefits for male employees, but not for female employees. Thus if a male employee dies while in service, his wife and children will be entitled to certain payments. If, however, a female employee dies while in service, her husband and/or children will not be entitled to any such payments. The employer could argue that this discrimination is permissible because it relates to death.

Dismissal

It is unlawful for your employer to discriminate against you by sacking you, or by adopting a selection procedure for redundancy which is discriminatory against women, or by having different compulsory retirement ages for men and women. For instance, if a company's redundancy selection procedure provides for the dismissal of part-timers first before applying the last in first out criterion, this may be indirect discrimination against women. Equally if a company has a compulsory retirement scheme whereby men are retired at the age of 65 and women at the age of 60 that would be unlawful discrimination.

If at the time of your dismissal you have worked for the same employer for at least two years, you will also be entitled to bring a claim for unfair dismissal. There is nothing to stop you claiming for both sex discrimination and unfair dismissal. The advantage of claiming for unfair dismissal as well is that in addition to the compensation you can get for sex discrimination, you can also ask to be reinstated or re-engaged in your old job.

Any other detriment

It is unlawful for your employer to discriminate against you by 'subjecting you to any detriment'. This simply means that employers act unlawfully if they do anything which puts women or married employees at a disadvantage. The mere fact that men and women are treated differently is not in itself sufficient; the differential treatment must in some way be to the disadvantage of either sex. Also you cannot complain of every small or trivial difference in treatment – it must be something serious or important.

There is no strict definition of the kind of treatment which amounts to a 'detriment'. Whether you have been subjected to a detriment will depend on all the circumstances of your individual case. A detriment exists if a reasonable worker would or might take the view that the treatment in question was to her detriment. The following are examples of what may constitute a 'detriment' if they are imposed on women employees and not on male

the employer may have a defence to your complaint, although the employee does not.

What is unlawful discrimination against 'contract workers'?

For the meaning of 'contract worker', see page 37.

It is unlawful for the 'principal' (your temporary employer) to discriminate against you on the grounds of your sex or marital status in any of the following ways:

(a) by allowing you to do your work on less favourable terms than men or single people in the same position;

(b) by not allowing you to do the work or to continue doing it. The 'principal' does not break the law if the work in question is such that being a man is a 'genuine occupational qualification' for the job (for the meaning of 'genuine occupational qualification' see page 40);

(c) by denying you access to any benefits, facilities or other services (whether provided by the principal or others), or by giving you restricted access to them. It may be that you are being denied or given restricted access as a member of the public as opposed to as a contract worker (see page 47). If you are discriminated against as a contract worker, you bring proceedings in the industrial tribunal. If, on the other hand, you are discriminated against as a member of the public, you bring proceedings in the County Court;

(d) by subjecting you to any other detriment (for the meaning of 'detriment', see page 49; for sexual harassment, see page 50).

Can employees of the Crown complain about sex discrimination?

Yes, they can because discrimination by the Crown as an employer is unlawful in exactly the same way as it is by a private employer. It is, therefore, unlawful for any Ministry, government department, statutory body or the holder of a statutory office to discriminate against women and married persons in relation to employment.

There are, however, two exceptions to this:

First, you cannot complain of sex discrimination in employment if the discrimination relates to the holding of a statutory office. A statutory office is one that is created by an Act of Parliament, and to which persons are appointed. For example, lay magistrates and adjudicators who hear immigration appeals are holders of statutory offices.

If a Minister of the Crown or a government department discriminates in making an appointment or in making the arrangements for determining who should be appointed to a particular office or post, the only course open to the aggrieved person is to apply to the High Court to review that decision.

Secondly, you cannot complain of sex discrimination in the armed forces. Thus discrimination is allowed in the army, navy, air force, their respective training cadet corps, and any women's service administered by the Defence Council.

Is sex discrimination in the police force unlawful?

Yes, it is, subject to the following three exceptions:

(a) it is lawful to discriminate between policemen and policewomen in requirements as to height, or uniform or equipment, or allowances in lieu of uniform or equipment;

(b) it is lawful to accord women special treatment in connection with pregnancy or childbirth; and

(c) it is lawful to discriminate in relation to pensions payable to special constables or police cadets.

In all other cases, it is unlawful for the police force to discriminate against policewomen and female police cadets in the same ways as it is for employers to discriminate against employees and potential employees. If you are a cadet or a policewoman, your employer is either the chief officer of police or the police authority, depending on which of the two has discriminated against you.

Proceedings for sex discrimination within the police force are brought in an industrial tribunal just as in any other employment case.

Can I do anything else to eliminate sex discrimination at my workplace?

If your workplace does not already have an equal opportunities policy, bring pressure upon your employer to formulate and adopt one. This does not mean simply stating that men and women are to be treated equally; your employer should lay down constructive policies aimed at wiping out sex discrimination, and should then take positive steps to implement them. If you are not sure about what should be included in a policy, obtain from the Equal Opportunities Commission (for address, see page 139) their *Code of Practice.* This provides guidance for employers about practices which should be adopted to provide equality. Having got your employer to adopt an equal opportunities policy, monitor it and make sure that steps are being taken to put it into practice.

What can I do if I have been discriminated against by an employer?

Proceedings for sex discrimination by employers are brought in industrial tribunals. Chapter 5 explains how to bring proceedings in an industrial tribunal and the bodies which can provide you with assistance to do so. It is important to remember that proceedings must be started within three months of the act of discrimination taking place. So if you feel that you have been the victim of discrimination, don't waste any time – seek advice immediately.

4: Discrimination in Other Fields of Employment

Is sex discrimination unlawful in other areas of employment?

Yes. Sex discrimination is unlawful in a wide variety of areas related to your working life. It is unlawful for the following to discriminate against you on the grounds of your sex or marital status: qualifying bodies (see below); training bodies (see pages 56–7); employment agencies and anyone else providing careers guidance (see pages 57–9); trade unions (see pages 59–61); professional and trade organizations (see pages 61–2); and partnerships (see page 62).

What is a 'qualifying body'?

A qualifying body is any organization or authority which has the power to grant, renew or extend any qualification or licence which you either need, or which makes it easier for you to engage in a particular profession or trade. The following are examples of qualifying bodies: the Law Society which regulates entry into the solicitors' profession, the British Medical Association which regulates entry into the medical profession, magistrates who grant licences to sell alcohol to publicans and those running restaurants, the Director of Fair Trading who licenses credit and hire businesses.

What is unlawful discrimination by a qualifying body?

A qualifying body acts unlawfully if it discriminates against you, as a woman or as a married person, by not granting you the licence or qualification for which you applied, by offering to grant it to you on less favourable terms than it does to men or single persons, or by withdrawing it from you.

If the qualifying body is required by law to satisfy itself as to the good character of the applicant before granting the relevant qualification or licence, it must take into account any evidence tending to show unlawful discrimination by the applicant or any of his employees or agents in the carrying on of any profession or trade. For instance, magistrates in deciding whether to renew a publican's licence should take into account any evidence which showed that he had discriminated against women customers by refusing to serve them.

It is, however, lawful for an organized religion to confer qualifications upon either men only or women only if it does so in order to comply with the doctrines of the religion or to avoid offending the religious susceptibilities of a significant number of its followers.

In some cases there is a right of appeal against the decision of the qualifying body. If such a right exists, then you must use it. If there is no right of appeal, you can bring proceedings against the qualifying body in an industrial tribunal.

What is a 'training body'?

For the purposes of sex discrimination the following are classified as 'training bodies':

(a) industrial training boards established by the Minister of Labour in order to provide training for jobs in commerce and industry to persons over compulsory school age;

(b) the Manpower Services Commission;

(c) any association of employers which has as its principal object, or as one of its principal objects, giving its employees access to training facilities.

What is unlawful discrimination by training bodies?

It is unlawful for a training body to discriminate against an actual or prospective female trainee by refusing her access to training courses or other facilities, by treating her less favourably than men in selecting her for training courses or in the type of training given, or by terminating her training.

Positive discrimination in training, however, is permitted in certain circumstances. If, in relation to particular work, it reasonably appears to anyone that at any time within the preceding twelve months there were either no women doing that work or the number of women doing it was comparatively small, then that person is allowed to restrict the training provided for that work to women only and to encourage women only to take advantage of opportunities for doing that work. A person may discriminate positively in this way if women are unrepresented or under-represented in that work in the country as a whole or just in a particular area. Thus an industrial training board would be entitled to send women only to training courses for plumbers if they took the view that there are comparatively few women plumbers in the country as a whole or in a particular area.

What is an 'employment agency'?

The term 'employment agency' refers to any person or organization which provides services (and that includes guidance on careers) for the purpose of finding jobs for workers or supplying employers with workers. It is irrelevant whether such services are provided free or for financial gain. The term, therefore, includes Job Centres, Careers Service offices, private agencies supplying temporary secretaries, a University Careers Service, and careers advisers in schools.

What is unlawful discrimination by an employment agency?

An employment agency acts unlawfully if it discriminates against a woman either by not providing her with any of its services or by treating her less favourably than a man in the provision of its services. This applies regardless of whether the woman in question is an employer looking for workers or a potential employee looking for work. Discrimination against married persons is unlawful in exactly the same way. The following are examples of unlawful sex discrimination by employment agencies:

A barristers' chambers looking for a clerk tells an employment agency that they are only interested in male candidates. Although the agency has suitably qualified women on its books, it does not send any of them for an interview.

A careers adviser in a school encourages the male students to become doctors, barristers and accountants, whereas the equally able female students are encouraged to go into the 'more caring' professions such as nurses, teachers and social workers. It is equally unlawful for employment agencies to have separate lists of available jobs for men and women based on stereotyped assumptions.

If you work in an employment agency and you are instructed by an employer to discriminate against women, report the matter at once to the Equal Opportunities Commission (for their address, see page 139). It is unlawful to instruct another person to discriminate, and it is something in respect of which the EOC can take action (see pages 134–136).

An employment agency does not, however, break the law if it does not send you for a job which the employer could lawfully refuse to offer you (see pages 40–4). Thus, for instance, if an employer could show that being a man is a genuine occupational qualification for a particular job, then an agency does not break the law by refusing to send women for that job.

An agency is also not liable for discrimination if it can prove that it acted reasonably in relying upon a statement made by the employers that they could lawfully refuse to offer a woman the job in question. If employers knowingly or recklessly make a false statement to this effect, they could be prosecuted in a magistrates' court and could be fined if convicted.

What is unlawful discrimination by trade unions?

It is unlawful for a trade union to discriminate against a woman wishing to join either by not accepting her application for membership or by offering her membership on less favourable terms than the male members. For example, it would be unlawful for a trade union to charge men and women different subscriptions, or to offer its male members higher rates of strike pay.

If you are already a member of a union it must not discriminate against you by depriving you of that membership or by treating you less favourably than the male members with regard to the benefits, facilities and services which it provides. These may include training facilities, social facilities, negotiations and assistance in disciplinary or dismissal procedures, legal services, and assistance during a strike.

Under English law, sex discrimination is permitted in respect of provisions made in relation to the death or retirement from work of a member. This may, however, be contrary to European law.

A union is also responsible in law for any acts of discrimination by its officers or shop stewards if they were acting on behalf of the union when such acts took place. In addition, the officer or shop steward will also be liable unless he can prove that he acted reasonably in relying upon a statement made by the union that the act in question would not be unlawful.

It is also unlawful for trade union members or representatives to persuade or induce, or to attempt to persuade or induce, employers to discriminate on the grounds of sex or marital status in the recruitment, promotion, transfer, training or dismissal of employees. This, however, is something in respect of which only the Equal Opportunities Commission can take action (see page 136).

Are trade unions allowed to discriminate positively?

Yes, trade unions may discriminate positively, that is, in favour of women, in the following three ways:

(a) if at any time within the preceding twelve months there were either no women holding a particular post in the union or the number of women holding such a post was comparatively small, the union is allowed to provide only its female members with training which would equip them for that post and to encourage its female members only to take advantage of opportunities for holding that post. This preferential treatment is limited to training women for, and encouraging them to apply for, a particular post. It is not, however, lawful, to discriminate in favour of women in making the actual appointment. Examples of this kind of positive discrimination would be holding shop stewards' courses for women only, or having a special campaign to recruit women officials;

(b) a trade union may have a special campaign to recruit women only if at any time within the preceding twelve months it either had no female members or the number of female members was comparatively small;

(c) a trade union may take steps to ensure that there is a minimum number of women on its elected committees. It may do this either by reserving a number of seats for women or by making extra seats available for women (by election or co-option or otherwise) when the number of women on the elected committee is below the minimum. No discrimination is allowed, however, in relation to the membership of the union or in determining who is entitled to vote.

What are professional and trade organizations?
A professional organization is one whose members carry out a particular profession, occupation or vocation for the purposes of which the organization exists. This includes such bodies as the Bar Council, the Law Society, the British Medical Association, the Royal Institute of British Architects, and the British Association of Social Workers.

A trade organization is one whose members carry out a particular trade or business for the purposes of which the organization exists.

Is sex discrimination by professional and trade organizations unlawful?
It is unlawful for a professional or trade organization to discriminate on the grounds of sex against existing and potential female members. It is unlawful to discriminate against potential members by refusing their applications for membership or by offering women membership on less favourable terms than those given to male members.

If a woman is already a member of such an organization, the organization acts unlawfully if it discriminates against her either by depriving her of her membership or by treating her less favourably than the male members, especially in relation to the benefits, facilities and services which it provides.

Professional and trade organizations are permitted to discriminate positively in favour of women by encouraging women only to join, by training and encouraging women only in connection with certain posts, and by reserving a certain minimum number of seats for women on their elected committees. The circumstances in which they can do this are exactly the same as those in which trade unions can discriminate positively (see page 60).

Is it unlawful for firms to discriminate against women partners?

Yes, it is. Most professionals such as doctors, dentists, solicitors, surveyors, accountants and architects operate as partnerships.

It is unlawful for a firm to discriminate against a woman applying to become a partner by making discriminatory arrangements for deciding who should be offered a partnership, by refusing to accept her as a partner or by offering to do so on less favourable terms than are afforded to the male partners. This applies to persons proposing to form themselves into a partnership just as it applies in relation to an existing firm. A firm can refuse to appoint women as partners if the position in question is such that being a man is a 'genuine occupational qualification' for the post (for the meaning of 'genuine occupational qualification' see page 40).

If a woman is already a partner in a firm, it is unlawful for the firm to discriminate against her in the provision of any of its benefits, facilities or services, or by expelling her from that position.

It is lawful to discriminate against women in provisions made in relation to death and retirement *unless* they relate to the expulsion of the woman from the partnership. Any discriminatory provisions relating to the woman ceasing to be a partner are unlawful. Thus it is unlawful for a firm to have different retirement ages for male and female partners. Under English law it may be lawful for the firm to pay different pension benefits to retired male and female partners. This may, however, be contrary to EEC law.

What can I do if I am discriminated against by any of the above?
You can bring proceedings for sex discrimination in an industrial tribunal (see chapter 5).

5: Proceedings in the Industrial Tribunal

Where do I bring proceedings for sex discrimination in the employment field?

All proceedings for sex discrimination relating to employment (that is, discrimination by any of the persons dealt with in chapters 3 and 4), and all claims for equal pay (see chapter 2) are brought in an industrial tribunal.

Every application should initially be sent to the Central Office of Industrial Tribunals (COIT), of which there are three; one in London (at 93 Ebury Bridge Road, London SW1. Tel: 01-730-9161) for England and Wales, one in Glasgow (at St Andrew's House, 141 West Nile Street, Glasgow G1 2RU. Tel: 041-331-1601) for Scotland, and one in Belfast (at Bedford House, 16–22 Bedford Street, Belfast BT2 7NR. Tel: 0232-327666) for Northern Ireland. The person to whom the applications must be sent is the Secretary of the Tribunals.

Once an application has been registered at the COIT, the Secretary then delegates it to the relevant Regional Office of Industrial Tribunals, which thereafter has charge of it. Regional offices have been established at Ashford, Birmingham, Bristol, Bury St Edmunds, Cardiff, Exeter, Leeds, London, Liverpool, Manchester, Newcastle-upon-Tyne, Nottingham, Sheffield and Southampton. Within each region, there is a certain number of centres where hearings take place.

At the hearing the tribunal will consist of three persons, a chairperson who will be either a solicitor or a barrister of at least seven years' standing and two non-lawyers. One of the two will have been appointed after consultation with employers' organizations, and the other after consultation with trade unions. The normal practice in sex discrimination cases is to make sure that the tribunal contains a female lay member. All three are equal members and they all participate in deciding the case, although the written decision will be signed only by the chairperson. The decision of the tribunal can be either unanimous or that of a majority.

A tribunal can proceed with a case if it consists of the chairperson and only one lay member, so long as both parties agree to it. If both parties do not agree, the hearing will have to be adjourned.

Each tribunal also has a clerk who is not a legally qualified person. The clerk will normally approach you before the hearing and explain the procedure and ask you for the names of your witnesses. He or she will be present throughout the hearing and at the end will advise you as to how you and your witnesses can claim expenses. Expenses which are allowed are loss of wages, travelling expenses and any other expenditure which you have incurred as a result of having to attend the hearing.

How do I start proceedings?

Proceedings before an industrial tribunal are started by sending an application to the Secretary of Tribunals at the relevant COIT. (For the addresses, see page 64).

There is a standard application form known as the 'IT1' for starting proceedings. This form is available from the COIT, Regional Offices of the Industrial Tribunals, employment exchanges and law centres. Although it is not essential to use this particular form, you should try to use it if you can obtain one.

If you cannot get hold of the form 'IT1' you can start proceedings simply by writing a letter to the Secretary of Tribunals at the COIT, stating in it your name and address, the name and address of the person about whom you are complaining and the grounds upon which you claim either to have been discriminated against or to be entitled to equal pay.

Although this appears to be simple enough, you should try and get legal advice before presenting your application. In some cases you may be entitled, in addition to claiming for sex discrimination, also to claim for race discrimination and/or unfair dismissal. Also it is important to try and make sure that you start proceedings against the right person. It may be the case that, although you work for a subsidiary company, your real employer is the parent company.

Are there any time limits within which I must bring proceedings?

There is no time limit for making a claim for equal pay under the Equal Pay Act, although you can only receive arrears of remuneration for two years preceding the date of your application (see page 34).

If you are complaining about sex discrimination, your application must be received at the COIT within three months of the act of discrimination taking place. If the act of discrimination continued over a certain period, then the time limit will begin to run from the end of that period. For example, a bookshop gives its male employees a special discount on books from the day on which they start their employment. Female employees are only given such a discount from their second year onwards. The three months, within which a woman employee must present her complaint for sex discrimination, would begin to run from the end of her first year in the job.

In calculating when the three-month period expires you must include the date on which the act of discrimination took place and remember that a month means an ordinary calendar month. Thus if you are discriminated against on the 6th of February your application must be received at the COIT by midnight on the 5th of May.

Where the discrimination relates to a dismissal, the date from which time begins to run is not the date when the notice of dismissal was given but the date on which the notice expired and your job effectively came to an end.

Even if the person about whom you are complaining does not take the point that your application was presented out of time, the tribunal itself may do so and refuse to hear your complaint.

The important thing is that your application must be delivered at the COIT office within the three-month period. It does not necessarily have to be handed over to anybody there. Thus, if the last day of your time limit falls on a Saturday, your application will have been presented in time if you push it through the letterbox of the COIT on that day. If the last day is a Saturday or a Sunday and it is at all possible for you to deliver it at the COIT on that day, do so – do not wait until the Monday. If, however, there is no letterbox or other means of getting your application into the building when the offices are closed, then the time limit will automatically be extended to the time when the offices open.

Don't rely on the postal service and post your application the day before the three-month time limit expires. Even with a first-class stamp, there is no guarantee that it will reach the COIT the following day.

If, however, you post your application three or four days in advance of the expiry date, but it is nevertheless delayed and arrives after the expiry date, the tribunal will determine as a preliminary issue whether it was in fact posted on the day that you say. If they come to the conclusion that it was, they will consider your application.

Are there any circumstances in which the industrial tribunal will extend the time limit?

A tribunal may hear your complaint of sex discrimination,

although it is out of time, if it considers that in all the circumstances of the case it would be 'just and equitable' to do so. The tribunal at this stage will not be concerned with the merits of your case (that is, whether you have a strong or a weak case) but with your reasons for not presenting your application in time.

In such a situation the tribunal will consider your knowledge, belief, experience and all the relevant circumstances. In some cases, the time limit may be extended because you did not know your rights or the time limit. However, if you had legal advice or access to legal advice, it is very unlikely that this will suffice. The decision in each case will depend on the individual concerned and the relevant facts.

If you are pursuing an appeal under the internal disputes procedure at your place of work, don't wait for the outcome of that before starting proceedings. Start proceedings within the three-month period.

What if I suspect that I have been discriminated against, but I need further information

If you think that you have been discriminated against, or know that you have, but require some further information in order to prepare your case, you can send to the discriminator a form asking certain questions. There is a standard form known as the 'Questionnaire of person aggrieved' which may be obtained free of charge from the Equal Opportunities Commission, or any local employment centre or job centre.

In this form you state your name and address and relate the facts which you think amount to discrimination. You then ask the person to whom it is sent whether he agrees with your version of events and, if not, in what respect he disagrees with it. You then ask him whether he accepts that his treatment of you was unlawful discrimination and, if not, ask him for his reasons for it and the extent to which consideration of your sex or marital status affected it. You may then ask any other questions which you think are relevant. For example, if you think that you were not offered a job because you are a woman, you can ask how many people applied for the job, how many of them were male, how many female, how many were interviewed or shortlisted and what their sex was, the sex of the successful applicant, the criteria used for selecting someone, how you fell short of the criteria, etc.

The questions asked by you and the replies given can be used as evidence in your case provided that they are served either before you present your application to the industrial tribunal or within 21 days of your doing so. If you wish to serve it any later and use it as evidence you will need the leave of the tribunal to do so.

If the discriminator does not reply to your questions, or gives answers which appear to be vague or evasive, the tribunal may draw from it whatever inference it wishes. It may well infer from that that the person concerned has discriminated unlawfully.

Another reason why it is useful to serve this form is that once the discriminator has given certain reasons for his behaviour, he is stuck with them. If he gives a different version or different reasons at the hearing, then this will cast a doubt upon his truthfulness and may well lead to the conclusion that he is lying because he has discriminated unlawfully.

Can I get any assistance for my case and, if so, will I have to pay for it?

The first thing to remember is that legal aid is not available for proceedings in an industrial tribunal. There is, however, a number of organizations and persons who can help you either by giving you advice or by preparing your case and representing you at the hearing without you having to pay for it.

The Equal Opportunities Commission (see also chapter 12). For address, see page 139.
The EOC can provide you with assistance (free of charge) in a variety of circumstances. If you want its help apply in writing, setting out as much detail as you can about the act of discrimination. Before reaching any decision the EOC will usually send out a questionnaire to the discriminator in order to get more information.

The EOC will agree to assist you if your case raises a question of principle and is likely to have wider effects than determining just your individual case. It will also provide assistance if it thinks that it is unrealistic for you to deal with the case without any help, either because it is a complex case or because of your position in relation to that of the discriminator. This would apply, for instance, where the discriminator is a rich and powerful organization and you are an individual without any resources. Finally, the EOC has a wide discretion to assist you if it feels that there is some special consideration in your case which merits it. In 1988, for instance, the EOC received 686 applications for assistance with proceedings in the tribunal. It provided assistance in 239 cases.

If the EOC decides to assist you, it can do so in a variety of ways. It may simply give you advice; it may take on your case, with one of its employees, who will be a qualified lawyer, acting on your behalf. This person will prepare the case and represent you at the hearing. It may send your case to a solicitor, who will then take over its conduct. The solicitor may deal with it personally or may engage a barrister. In any case, you will be legally represented at the hearing.

If the EOC agrees to assist you, it won't cost you a penny and you will get qualified lawyers taking on your case. The only problem is that it takes the EOC quite some time to reach a decision and you may suddenly be told at a fairly late stage that you are not getting any help.

Free Representation Unit
3 Middle Temple Lane, London EC4Y 9AA.
Telephone 01-353-3697
FRU does not take on cases directly, but receives referrals from Citizens' Advice Bureaux and law centres. If it receives your case at an early stage, it will help you prepare it and advise you on settling it. If it receives it at a later stage, it will provide someone to represent you at the tribunal. In either event, it won't cost you anything. The person who will represent you will be a barrister or a solicitor or someone training to be a barrister or a solicitor, or a law student. Although he or she may not be a qualified lawyer, he or she will probably have had some experience of industrial tribunal cases. As FRU relies on lawyers volunteering their services, it cannot always guarantee representation, but provides it in about 70% of the cases referred to it.

Trade unions
If you belong to a trade union, your shop steward or union official may be able to help you bring your case and represent you at the hearing.

Law centres
Find out if there is a law centre in your area (look under 'Law Centres' in the phone directory, or phone the Law Centres Federation at 01-387-8570) and go and see them. They will be able to provide you with free advice, assistance and representation for your case.

Citizens' Advice Bureaux
Find the nearest Citizens' Advice Bureau to you (look in

the phone directory under 'Citizens' Advice Bureaux'). It is advisable to call first, as they do not always open during normal working hours. They will be able to advise you on the merits of your case and how to start proceedings. They will also be able to refer you to some other organizations which could provide you with assistance and representation.

Solicitors
Solicitors can provide free or partly free advice under something known as the 'green form scheme'. Under this, the solicitor can advise you on the merits of your case, help you in filling out your originating application and advise you as to the evidence you will need to back up your claim. However, he or she is not covered by this to represent you at the tribunal and, therefore, cannot provide you with free representation. If he or she appears for you at the tribunal and conducts your case for you, you will be charged for it.

What if the other side refuses to allow me to see documents which are relevant to the case?
The other side does not *have* to show you any documents unless you obtain a formal order for discovery from the industrial tribunal. You can apply for this either before the hearing by giving notice of it to the Secretary of the Tribunals or at the hearing itself. The tribunal can then order the other side to give you copies of the relevant documents or to allow you to inspect them, and they will impose a time limit by which the order is to be complied with.

The tribunal may order discovery of documents which are or have been in the other side's possession and relate to any question in the proceedings. The criterion used in deciding to make such an order is whether it is necessary for disposing fairly of the proceedings or for saving costs.

If the documents which you want to look at contain confidential information or relate to persons who are not directly involved in the proceedings, the tribunal can still allow you to see them, but may take steps to cover up or blackout names and certain other matters. For example, you complain of discrimination because you were not promoted to a certain post and you want to see the application forms of the other applicants, and the personnel records and assessments of those of them who work in the same office as you. The tribunal will probably order that their names and addresses should not be disclosed, but that you are entitled to see details of their qualifications and experience, and assessments of their work.

If a person against whom an order for discovery is made does not comply with it, the tribunal may strike out his notice of appearance (the document containing his defence to your allegations) in whole or in part and, where appropriate, may even stop him from opposing your application altogether. However, the tribunal can only do this if, after the time limit for compliance with the order has expired, they send that person a notice and give him every opportunity to tell them why such a course should not be adopted.

Do conciliation officers become involved at all?

Once you present your application to the industrial tribunal, the Secretary will send copies of all the relevant papers to a conciliation officer. The conciliation officer then usually contacts both sides and offers his services. If both parties want his help, or if he thinks that he can act with a reasonable prospect of success, it is his duty to try to resolve the matter without it having to go to the industrial tribunal. If you wish, you can ask for the assistance of a conciliation officer before presenting your claim.

If you are still in employment and have not yet started proceedings, the conciliation officer will usually encourage you to use any internal procedures that are available at your place of work. If you decide to follow this course, keep in mind the date by which you must start proceedings (see page 66).

Anything that is said or written to a conciliation officer in connection with the performance of his duties cannot be used as evidence at the hearing without the agreement of the person who wrote or said it.

If a conciliation officer becomes involved, he should take a neutral stand and his role should simply be to help you and the discriminator reach some kind of an agreement.

Where a settlement is reached with the help of a conciliation officer, it will usually contain an agreement not to pursue the matter in an industrial tribunal. Once you have accepted such a settlement, you cannot start or continue with proceedings in the industrial tribunal in respect of the same matter.

In what circumstances should I settle a case?

'Setting a case' means reaching an agreement with your employer whereby he agrees to offer you a certain sum of money and/or other undertakings which you seek, in return for you undertaking not to pursue your claim. This can happen at any stage before the hearing starts at the tribunal, or in the course of the hearing itself. It may involve a joint statement signed by both parties or their representatives. The discriminator will never accept that he has discriminated, and may wish specifically to deny having discriminated, even though he is offering you money.

Before deciding whether or not to accept a settlement, take legal advice as to the strength of your case and the amount of damages that a tribunal is likely to award you (for damages, see pages 82–4). If you do not have a very strong case and you think that you may have difficulty in proving discrimination, it is advisable to accept a settlement. But remember you are not stuck with the figure that the discriminator has mentioned; you can negotiate with him. The better your case, the stronger your bargaining position. If you have a very strong case, the discriminator may be willing to offer you more than a tribunal will award you. Push him as high as you can. In a case like that, the discriminator will often be more concerned about the adverse publicity that a finding of discrimination will bring, than the money he has to give you. He may try to make you accept formally that there was no discrimination and that the details of the settlement should not be made public. In most cases, it would be better not to accept either of those terms.

In some cases you may still be in the job where the discrimination took place. If that is the case, then try to have the settlement include an undertaking by your employer not to victimize you for bringing proceedings for sex discrimination. It is, of course, illegal for him to do so, but having an undertaking to that effect emphasizes the point. If there is no equal opportunities policy at your workplace, try to get your employer to undertake as part of the settlement that such a policy will be formulated and adopted.

The terms on which you settle your case will depend on the facts and circumstances surrounding it. For instance, in a promotion case, you may get your employer to undertake that you will be offered the relevant post when next a vacancy arises for it. It is important, however, that you remember that getting a good deal for yourself should not be the only consideration; try to ensure, so far as is possible, that other persons will not suffer the same discrimination that you did.

How do I prepare for the hearing?

You will be given at least 14 days' notice of the place and

date of the hearing. Make sure that anyone who can support your account is available to give evidence on the day of the hearing. If any of your witnesses are not available, take a signed, written statement from the person or persons in question. This can be used in evidence although it will not carry the same weight as the witness giving evidence in person. If you intend to rely on a written statement, you must send copies of it at least seven days before the hearing to the Secretary of the Tribunals and to the other side. If the unavailable witness is very important to your case, try writing to the Secretary well in advance and ask if your hearing can be moved to another date.

The other important thing is the documents on which you intend to rely or refer to in the course of the hearing. These may include a newspaper advertisement, your application for a job, your contract of employment, a letter from the employer dismissing you, a certificate of your qualifications, etc. Make photocopies of all the relevant documents, including your originating application, the other side's notice of appearance, a questionnaire, if any was sent, and the answer to it, and clip them all together. Number the documents and make an index listing the documents and the pages at which they are to be found. This is your 'bundle'. Make sure that you have six copies of the bundle. Send one to the other side before the hearing; they may wish to add nothing to it, in which case it becomes an 'agreed bundle', or they may prefer to prepare a bundle of their own. Three copies will be required for the tribunal; these may be handed to the clerk on the day of the hearing. One will be your copy, and the last one can be used by witnesses when giving evidence.

What is the procedure at the hearing?

Proceedings in an industrial tribunal are, on the whole,

less formal than in a court of law. You can either appear yourself or be represented by a solicitor, a barrister, a representative of your trade union or anyone else that you want.

As it is upon you to prove discrimination, you or your representative will open the case and call your evidence first. 'Opening a case' simply means giving a brief outline of your case with reference to the documents in your bundle. Then you give your evidence and call any witnesses who support your case. It is entirely a matter for you to decide in what order you call your witnesses and it is your duty to ensure that all the relevant evidence is before the tribunal. The other side will cross-examine your witnesses, and in doing so will put to them the facts on which they rely. Once you have called all your evidence, it will be upon the other side to call their witnesses, and you will be entitled to cross-examine them. At the end of the evidence, both sides will have an opportunity to sum up their respective cases.

If you are not represented, the tribunal will explain to you the procedure and the relevant law and will generally help you to present your case. However, they will not tell you what evidence to call, nor will they cross-examine the other side's witnesses for you. As far as your evidence is concerned, they will either allow you to give your account without being interrupted or will ask you questions and treat your answers as your evidence.

At the end of the hearing, the tribunal may give you its decision there and then, or it may decide later on. In any event, it will send you its decision in writing and the reasons for reaching that decision.

How do I prove direct discrimination?

You will have to prove to the tribunal, first, that you were treated less favourably than a man or a single person was, or would have been, treated and, secondly, that it is more likely than not that the reason for it was your sex or marital status. It is extremely difficult to find hard concrete evidence of sex discrimination. A person who discriminates against you on the grounds of your sex is hardly likely to put that forward as a way of explaining his behaviour.

Tribunals are well aware of the difficulties of proving sex discrimination and, therefore, adopt the following approach when determining cases. Once a tribunal is satisfied that you were treated less favourably than a man or a single person, it will then look carefully at the reasons given for it by the discriminator. For example, if you prove that a male colleague less qualified and suitable than you was promoted instead of you, or that an employer told you that you were not suitable for a job once it was discovered that you were married, then you have proved that you were treated less favourably. It is then for the employer to provide an explanation. In the absence of any explanation, or of a satisfactory and credible explanation, the tribunal is entitled to conclude that you were unlawfully discriminated against on the grounds of your sex or marital status. The fact that the employer denies that your sex was a relevant consideration in deciding who was appointed or promoted is not in itself enough. Employers have to give clear and concise reasons for their behaviour. If the tribunal accepts their reasons as genuine, then your claim will be dismissed. If not, you will succeed.

If the discriminator has deliberately and without reasonable excuse failed to reply to the questionnaire sent by you (see page 68), or his answers have been vague or evasive, the tribunal may infer from that that he has unlawfully discriminated against you.

You can rely on acts of discrimination in the past in respect of which no proceedings were brought and for which the time limit has already expired in order to show that the act about which you are complaining was sex discrimination. For example, in July 1989 your application for promotion is turned down although you are a suitable candidate for it. A male colleague with less qualification and experience than you is promoted instead. You can bring evidence to show that the same thing happened in July 1988, and rely on it to show that you were discriminated against in July 1989.

You can also produce evidence about things which happened *after* the act about which you are complaining in order to show that that act was discriminatory. For instance, in the above example, you could produce evidence to show that the person responsible for deciding who should be promoted said to someone else in August or September 1989 that women were all right in clerical posts but were not assertive or confident enough for more senior management posts. The purpose of bringing in that evidence would be to show that the person in question had not promoted you because of his stereotypical assumptions about women. It would then be upon him to explain his sexist remarks.

You can also rely on statistical evidence relating to the workforce as a whole. For example, you are a Grade IV employee, complaining about discrimination in not being promoted to Grade III. You can ask the tribunal to infer sex discrimination from the fact that, although about half the Grade IV employees are women, no woman has been promoted to Grade III in the past five years. This kind of information is not always easy to obtain, so make sure that in preparing your case you have used the questionnaire procedure (see page 68) and discovery (see page 72).

How do I prove indirect discrimination?

In order to prove indirect discrimination you have to prove three things. First, that the discriminator has imposed a particular requirement or condition, which applies to everyone regardless of sex or marital status. Secondly, that you cannot comply with it and, thirdly, that the proportion of women or married persons who can comply with it is considerably smaller than the proportion of men or single persons who can comply with it (see pages 5–7). The rest of this answser deals with discrimination against women, although the same, of course applies to discrimination against married persons.

It is extremely important that you clearly define the requirement or condition which you say was applied in your case (see page 7). This is not always easy to do, and it is best to get the advice of a lawyer before you do so.

The most complicated part to prove in an indirect discrimination case is that the proportion of women who can comply with a requirement or condition is smaller than the proportion of men. In order to do so, one does not necessarily compare all the women in the country with all the men. It is necessary to define a 'pool', that is, a section of the community within which the comparison must be made. The pool must be such that the relevant circumstances of the men and women being compared are either the same or not materially different. What constitutes the pool in any given case will depend on the facts of that case. For example, an employer imposes a requirement for a job that all applicants must be under 30. The only qualification necessary for the job is that applicants must have at least two A Levels. The pool in such a case would be all men and women who have the necessary qualification for the job. The pool would, however, be different if, for example, the discrimination relates to the redundancy procedures at a particular workplace. The employer stipulates that all part-timers will be made redundant before the normal 'last in first out' rule applies. In such a case, the pool would be all the men and women workers at that workplace.

Although one would have thought that a tribunal would accept, without evidence being produced, that women generally assume responsibility for childcare, and therefore that a smaller proportion of them can comply with a requirement to work full-time or when under the age of 30, this is not always the case. You should, therefore, always try to produce statistical evidence to this effect.

You also have to prove that the proportion of women who can comply with the requirement or condition is 'considerably smaller' than the proportion of men who can comply with it. There is no strict rule as to what the difference must be between the percentages of women and men who can comply with it for it to be accepted as 'considerably smaller'.

Once you have proved the above, it is then for the discriminator to show that the condition or requirement was justifiable (see page 8). If he cannot show it to be justifiable, you will succeed in your claim.

What can the tribunal do if I prove discrimination?

Once the tribunal is satisfied that you were discriminated against it may do one of the following two things:

(a) the Tribunal may recommend that the discriminator takes certain action within a specified period for the purpose of removing or reducing the adverse effect which the discrimination had on you. Thus, if a tribunal finds that you were not promoted to a particular position because of sex discrimination, it may recommend that you are promoted to that position as soon as there is a vacancy for it. The tribunal can only make a recommendation which relates to you personally; it cannot make a general recommendation in order to eradicate discriminatory practices. If the discriminator does not follow the tribunal's recommendation, the tribunal may award you money if none has been awarded so far, or it may increase the sum originally awarded;

(b) the tribunal can award you a sum of money. The amount of money awarded will depend upon the circumstances of your particular case and the loss, if any, which you have suffered. There are three particular matters in respect of which the tribunal can award you money:

(i) injury to feelings. This is money given to you for the offence and distress caused to you by the act of discrimination. It varies according to the circumstances in which the discrimination took place, but is usually in the region of £500. Higher awards in the region of £2,000–£3,000 have been given in some cases of sexual harassment.

(ii) loss of job opportunity. This is generally awarded when you are not offered a job because of sex discrimination. Whether any money is awarded, and the amount which is given, depends on a number of factors – your qualifications and experience, the type of job applied for, the general availability of jobs of that kind and how certain it was that you would have got the job had it not been for the discrimination. The more scarce and specialized the job, the higher the award of damages. For example, if you are not offered the position of consultant neurosurgeon, the damages will be considerable. If, on the other hand, the job in question is a clerical job and one which requires no qualification or special skills, you will get hardly any money for loss of job opportunity.

(iii) Loss of earnings. This is normally awarded where the discrimination relates to a dismissal and is intended to compensate you for the financial loss caused by the dismissal.

In calculating your loss, you use as the starting point your net pay, that is what you used to receive after tax and national insurance deductions. You also include and take into account regular overtime which you did, any bonus payments and fringe benefits.

Remember that it is your duty to act reasonably after your dismissal and to do whatever you can to decrease your loss. Thus you should make every effort to find another job. Keep a record of your efforts to do so and also copies of any relevant documents (i.e. advertisements which you answered, job applications, letters from employers, etc.). The tribunal would probably consider it unreasonable for you to refuse another similar job simply because it does not pay as well as your old one. If the tribunal feels that you did not make any effort to find another job, or that you unreasonably refused to accept one that was offered, they will reduce the amount of money awarded to you.

In deciding the amount of money to give you for loss of earnings, the tribunal will take it in two stages. First, the loss of earnings between the date of dismissal and the date of hearing and, secondly, the future loss of earnings.

The first is relatively easy to work out – it is the net amount you would have earned in your old job minus the amount you have actually earned in your new job, or should have earned had you taken steps to reduce your loss. If you earn more in your new job, then the extra earnings in the new job will be set off against your loss.

The second is more difficult to work out and involves guesswork to a large extent. If by the time of the hearing you have a new job and it pays less than your old one, the future loss of earnings will be the difference between the two net wages for a specified period of time in the future. If the new job pays more than the old, then there is no future loss of earnings.

If you do not have a new job by the date of the hearing, it becomes more complicated. In assessing how much to award, the tribunal will take into account such matters as when you are likely to get a new job and how much you are likely to earn in that job. This depends, of course, on your qualifications and skills and the local employment situation.

At the time of going to press, in September 1989, the maximum amount of money the tribunal can give you is £8,925. If you claim for sex discrimination and/or unfair dismissal, the maximum you can get as compensation is still the same. If you claim for unfair dismissal you will be entitled, in addition, to a basic award. In an unfair dismissal case, you are also entitled to ask to be re-engaged or reinstated in your old job.

If your complaint was about indirect discrimination and the tribunal finds that it is proved, it cannot award you any money if the discriminator proves that the requirement or condition in question was not applied with the *intention* of discriminating against you.

Will I have to pay the other side's costs if I lose?

Usually, no. It is only in exceptional circumstances that the tribunal will ask you to pay the other side's costs. It will only do so if in bringing or conducting your case you have acted 'frivolously', 'vexatiously' or otherwise unreasonably. You will have acted 'frivolously' if you brought your claim knowing that there was no substance in it and it was bound to fail. You will have acted 'vexatiously' if you brought a hopeless claim, not because you thought you might win but out of spite to harass someone or for some other improper motive.

In deciding whether you should be ordered to pay the other side's costs, the tribunal will take into account your ability, or the lack of it, to meet such an order. If an order is made against you, it will usually be for a fixed sum.

The only other instance in which you may be ordered to pay the other side's costs is if the hearing has to be adjourned because of you. Whether you are so ordered will depend on the reasons for the adjournment. If, for example, you apply at the hearing to amend your application by adding new details to it, and the other side asks for an adjournment because it needs time to consider the new allegations, then you will have to pay the other side's costs for attending on that day. If, however, the adjournment is due to something completely unforeseen and not in any way your fault, then you won't have to pay the other side's costs. For example, you fall ill and are taken to hospital the night before the hearing.

If you are assisted by the EOC and are ordered to pay costs, the EOC will do so and you won't have to pay.

If you win the case and the tribunal is of the opinion that the discriminator has acted frivolously, vexatiously or otherwise unreasonably in defending the case, they can order him to pay your legal costs if you have incurred any. Similarly, if the case has to be adjourned because of the discriminator doing something at a late stage, he will have to pay your legal costs for attending on that day.

Is the procedure different in equal pay cases?

If your claim is on the basis that you are engaged on like work or equivalently rated work, then the procedure is the same as in a sex discrimination case, save in the following respects:

(a) there is no time limit within which proceedings must be brought (see page 66);

(b) you cannot send out the EOC questionnaire to obtain further information (see page 68); and

(c) there is a difference as to what the tribunal will grant you if you win your case (see page 34).

Otherwise, proceedings are started and conducted in the same way. It will be upon you to produce evidence of the fact that you are engaged on like work or equivalently rated work as a man. In a particularly large workforce, it may be difficult for you to identify the man with whom you ought to compare yourself without having access to the details of the other employees. In such a case you may apply to the tribunal to have sight of and inspect documents which are in the possession of the employer (see page 72). Once you have proved that you are engaged on like work or equivalently rated work, it will then be for your employer to prove that the variation in wages is genuinely due to a material difference other than the difference in sex (see page 29).

If your claim is on the basis that you are doing work which is of equal value to that of a man, then in addition to the differences stated above, there is a special procedure in the tribunal for determining the claim (see page 28).

What do I get if I win my equal pay case?

See page 34. Costs are awarded in the same circumstances as in a sex discrimination case (see page 85).

Can I appeal if I lose my case?

Yes, but only if you can show one or more of the following:

(a) that the tribunal misdirected itself in law, or misunderstood the law, or misapplied the law;

(b) that the tribunal misunderstood or misapplied the facts;

(c) that the decision of the tribunal was perverse or that there was no evidence to justify the conclusion which was reached. In order to show that a decision was perverse you would have to show that no tribunal, having applied the law correctly, could have reached that decision. It is not enough to show that the tribunal relied on evidence which was hard to believe.

You appeal from an industrial tribunal to the Employment Appeal Tribunal; the central office is at 4 St James' Square, London SW1Y 4JB. (Tel: 01-214-3367). The important thing to remember is that, unlike a case in the industrial tribunal, you can get legal aid for bringing or defending proceedings in the Employment Appeal Tribunal (EAT). As proceedings in the EAT involve legal arguments it is better to engage a lawyer than to try to conduct them yourself.

You start the appeal proceedings by sending to the EAT a Notice of Appeal and a copy of the written reasons of the industrial tribunal's decision. The time limit for appealing is 42 days from the day on which the written reasons for the decision were sent to you. If you appeal after the 42-day period has expired, your Notice of Appeal must be accompanied by an application for extension of time, setting out the reasons for the delay. You will only be allowed to appeal out of time in exceptional circumstances and it will depend primarily on whether you have a good excuse for the delay. It will not necessarily be a good excuse to say that the reason for the delay is that legal aid was not granted within the 42-day period, or that you were trying to get assistance from the EOC, your trade union or some other body.

If, on reading the Notice of Appeal, the EAT feels that there is no arguable point of law, it may set the case for a hearing on a preliminary point. It will then be for the person appealing to show why the appeal should not be dismissed. If the appellant fails in this, the appeal will be dismissed. If he/she succeeds, the appeal will be set down for a hearing and will be heard at a later date. There will be a similar hearing on a preliminary point if the appeal depends solely or mainly on the ground that the tribunal took an erroneous view of the evidence or reached an unreasonable conclusion upon the facts. These are fairly short hearings and generally do not take more than an hour.

You will have to send to the EAT documents which were before the tribunal *and* are relevant to the appeal. There is no need to send *all* the documents which were used before the tribunal.

At the beginning of each month the EAT publishes a

list of all the cases to be heard in the following month. You will be notified as soon as your case appears on the list. If you cannot attend on the date given to you, you may apply to the listing office to have the date altered, but must do so before the fifteenth of the month in which the case appeared in the list.

At the hearing of the appeal you can appear in person or be represented by lawyers or any other person of your choice.

The person who loses the appeal will not normally have to pay the other side's costs unless the EAT considers that the proceedings were unnecessary, improper or vexatious or that there has been an unreasonable delay or other unreasonable conduct in bringing or conducting the proceedings. The kind of case in which you would normally have to pay costs is where the appeal was not based on any point of law and you abandon it on the day of the hearing or shortly before it.

You can appeal on a question of law from the EAT to the Court of Appeal. In order to do so you have to get the leave of either the EAT or the Court of Appeal. The time limit for appealing to the Court of Appeal is four weeks from the date of the decision of the EAT.

6: Education

In what areas of education is sex discrimination unlawful?

There are three aspects of education in which sex discrimination is against the law. First, it is unlawful for schools to discriminate against a child on the grounds of the child's sex. This applies equally to primary and secondary schools, and regardless of whether the school in question is a state school maintained by a local education authority, or an independent school (better known as a 'public' school), or a special school. Special schools are for children who have special needs, such as children who are blind, deaf, educationally subnormal, severely physically handicapped or maladjusted. Some special schools are maintained by local education authorities and are free, others are independent and fee-paying.

Secondly, it is unlawful for a large number of institutions which provide further education to discriminate against you on the grounds of your sex.

Thirdly a local education authority must not discriminate on the grounds of sex in the carrying out of any of its functions.

All of these provisions are explained more fully in the rest of this chapter.

Is it lawful to have single-sex educational establishments?

Yes it is. A 'single-sex establishment' means a school or college which either admits pupils of one sex only or generally admits pupils of one sex only but has exceptionally admitted some pupils of the opposite sex or has a comparatively small number of pupils of the other sex whose admission is confined to particular courses of instruction or teaching classes. A single-sex school or college acts lawfully if it refuses to admit members of the other sex. If the establishment does make an exception and admits a member of the opposite sex, it would then be breaking the law if it discriminated against that pupil on the grounds of his or her sex. If, however, the admission of a pupil of the opposite sex is confined to a particular course, then the school or college does not break the law by refusing that pupil access to other courses.

The following examples indicate what this means:

A boys' school acts lawfully if it refuses to admit any girls.

A girls' primary school, which admits boys to the kindergarten only, acts lawfully if it refuses to admit boys to the primary school. It would be breaking the law, however, if it discriminated in any way against the boys which it had admitted to the kindergarten.

A boys' school admits two female pupils to take an A Level course in Physics. The school acts lawfully if it refuses to allow the girls to attend any other classes in the school. It also remains a single-sex school and does not break the law by refusing to admit girls generally to the school.

What is unlawful discrimination by a co-educational school?

It is unlawful for a mixed school to discriminate against a girl applying to the school either by not admitting her, or by offering to do so on less favourable terms than the boys. For example, a mixed secondary school which has 300 places in the first year applies a quota limiting the number of girls to be admitted to 100. Your daughter is refused admission to the school because the quota has already been filled. The school has unlawfully discriminated against your daughter because the only reason for refusing to admit her is the fact that she is a girl. Similarly, a school acts unlawfully if it offers to admit a girl but restricts her choice of subjects by saying, for instance, that she cannot study any science subjects because the majority of boys has chosen them and there is no more room in those classes for her.

If your daughter is already attending a mixed school, it is unlawful for the school to discriminate against her by not allowing her to attend certain classes or courses, or by refusing her access to any other benefits, facilities or services which it provides, by expelling her or by treating her in any way less favourably than the male pupils. The following are examples of unlawful sex discrimination:

Your daughter's class is divided on Friday afternoons into two groups. All the boys attend a craft and technology class. All the girls attend a home economics class. Your daughter wants to go to the craft and technology class, but is told that she cannot because that is for boys only. The school is unlawfully discriminating against your daughter.

Your daughter's year in her school is divided into three classes, A, B and C. The class which any child enters depends on the subjects the child wishes to take and his or her ability to do them. Your daughter wishes to go to Class B and has the ability to do the subjects taught in that class. She is, however, told that she cannot enter that class although boys with less ability than her are allowed to. The school has a policy of ensuring a balance between male and female pupils in each class. The reason your daughter and other girls are not allowed to go to Class B is that it would lead to an imbalance between the sexes in that class. The school is unlawfully discriminating against your daughter.

Your daughter attends a mixed secondary school and the school refuses to allow her to play football or cricket, insisting that these are 'boys' sports'. That is unlawful discrimination by the school.

There are certain circumstances in which sex discrimination is permitted by schools (for these see page 95).

Can I do anything about sexist attitudes and books in a school?

Most discrimination in education stems from stereotypical assumptions and from differing attitudes towards and expectations of male and female pupils. Recent statistics show that the percentage of girls opting for arts subjects is still far greater than the percentage choosing to study the sciences or mathematics. This is because girls have traditionally always been encouraged to take arts subjects, and it is very difficult to change patterns and traditions which have become deeply entrenched over a very long time.

The problem is that you can only bring legal proceedings for a specific act of discrimination which you can clearly identify, such as your daughter being refused the option to take physics and chemistry as A level subjects. You cannot, however, take any legal action because a school does nothing to change existing patterns and does not take any steps to encourage girls to study physics or chemistry. Nor can you bring legal proceedings in respect of teachers' sexist attitudes and expectations, or the use of sexist books.

The only way in which you as parents can get anything done is by keeping in close contact with the school, being aware of what is going on, liaising with other parents and teachers, making formal complaints and letting your objections be known to whoever is responsible for the school. You can also influence the policy of the school by getting on to the board of governors or managers, or by electing another parent who shares your views.

If you are a teacher and opposed to the use of sexist books and sexist traditions and patterns in education, you should raise it with other teachers at staff meetings and try to enlist the support of your union. It is important to remember that discrimination is not eradicated simply by making particular subjects and options formally available to boys and girls on equal terms. In order to change existing patterns it is necessary to take some positive steps. For example, teachers in primary schools should ensure that play activities, displays and the books used do not reinforce traditional sex roles either in the workforce or at home. Teachers in secondary schools should carefully explain to pupils the educational and career implications of particular choices before pupils decide on the subjects which they wish to take.

What can a teacher or headmistress do if the school discriminates against her?

If you are a teacher or a headmistress and the school discriminates against you in relation to recruitment, promotion or dismissal, you are suffering from discrimination as an employee. You can, therefore, bring proceedings for it in an industrial tribunal against your employer. Your employer will be either the local education authority, or the governors or managers of the school, depending on who was responsible for the relevant act of discrimination (see chapters 3 and 5).

Parents and students can, of course, support the teacher by organizing a campaign and bringing pressure to bear upon the school and the local education authority.

Who can be held responsible for sex discrimination in schools?

If the school in question is maintained by a local education authority, the body responsible for sex discrimination will be the local education authority or the managers or governors of the school, depending on whose duty it was to carry out the act about which you are complaining.

If the school is an independent school or a special school which is not maintained by a local education authority, the person responsible will be the proprietor, that is, the person or body of persons responsible for the management of the school.

In either case, the relevant body will also be responsible for any acts of discrimination by any of its employees, i.e. the headmaster or headmistress or teachers, unless it can show that it took such steps as were reasonably practicable to stop the person in question behaving in a discriminatory fashion.

What is unlawful sex discrimination in further education?

'Further education' covers a large number of institutions that provide education, training or instruction for those who have left school. It includes universities, polytechnics, colleges, medical schools in hospitals, teachers' training colleges and other educational establishments maintained by local education authorities or funded by the Department of Education and Science. It is irrelevant whether the establishment provides full-time or part-time education. Any reference to a university includes its colleges and halls.

It is unlawful for any of the above institutions to discriminate against you on the grounds of your sex either by not offering you a place or by offering to do so on less favourable terms than those offered to the male students. For example, you apply to a college to study engineering and technology. Part of the course involves practical training for which you have to be placed within certain firms. The college does not accept you for that course because they believe it would be difficult to obtain training placements for women. The only reason that the college has refused to offer you a place is because you are a woman and that is unlawful sex discrimination. If the college offered you a place subject to you making your own arrangements to obtain a training placement (although the college would be responsible for making these arrangements for the male students), it is offering you a place on less favourable terms than those offered to the men, and that would amount to unlawful discrimination.

If you are already a student at one of these institutions, it is unlawful for the institution to discriminate against you on the grounds of your sex by not allowing you to take certain courses or attend certain classes, by refusing you or restricting your access to any of the benefits, facilities and services which are provided, or by treating you unfavourably in any other way. This means that discrimination is illegal not only on the academic front, but also in other aspects of your life at the institution.

Although universities and colleges are entitled to provide separate accommodation for men and women (see page 128), the accommodation provided to each sex must be of a similar standard. It would be acting unlawfully if, for instance, washing machines were installed in male halls of residence but not in the female ones.

Are there any circumstances in which discrimination in education is permitted?

Yes, sex discrimination is allowed in the following circumstances:

(a) single-sex educational establishments (see page 89);

(b) boarders in schools: a co-educational school (one with pupils of both sexes) which admits both boarders and day-pupils is entitled to restrict the admission of boarders and the provision of boarding facilities to members of one sex only. Thus a mixed school in which all the boarders are boys, or which has a comparatively small number of girl boarders, acts lawfully if it refuses to admit girls as boarders;

(c) single-sex establishments turning co-educational: any single-sex establishment (or mixed school with single-sex boarding facilities) which wants to turn co-educational over a period of time may apply for what is known as a 'transitional exemption order'. In the case of public sector establishments the application is made to the appropriate Education Minister, and in the case of private sector establishments to the Equal Opportunities Commission. If such an order is granted it will allow the school or college to discriminate in its admissions policy for a specified period. Any discrimination in relation to admission between the making of the application for the order and the determination of the application is also lawful. Hence a girls' schools which wants to become mixed will be entitled to reserve a certain number of places for boys only during the period specified in the order;

(d) educational charities: any discrimination which results from following the terms of a charitable trust is lawful. For example, a trust provides scholarships for boys going to Cambridge University. You cannot complain of sex discrimination on the ground that the scholarship is available to boys only. It is, however, open to the trustees in such a case (if they so wish) to apply to the Education Minister to be allowed to offer the scholarships to girls as well;

(e) physical training: any discrimination which takes place in relation to a further education course in physical training is lawful;

(f) see also chapter 10 for the general exceptions.

What is unlawful discrimination by local education authorities?

It is unlawful for a local education authority to discriminate on the grounds of sex in the carrying out of any of its functions. Local education authorities perform a large variety of functions, some of which are compulsory, others discretionary. It is impossible to set out here all the functions of local education authorities, but the following are perhaps the most relevant for the purposes of sex discrimination.

Local education authorities have a duty to ensure that primary and secondary schools in their area are sufficient in number, character and equipment to give all pupils opportunities for education offering such variety of instruction and training as may be desirable in view of their different ages, abilities and aptitudes, including practical instruction and training appropriate to their respective needs.

Local education authorities also have a duty to ensure that the facilities for further education in their areas are adequate for the full-time and part-time education of persons over compulsory school age, and also for leisure-time occupation for such persons who are able and willing to profit by the facilities provided for that purpose.

Furthermore, local education authorities are also responsible for awarding discretionary grants for further education.

The following are examples of unlawful sex discrimination by local education authorities:

Your daughter goes to a local girls' secondary school, your son to a local boys' secondary school. Both are state schools maintained by the same local education authority. Your daughter's school does not have any physics or chemistry laboratories, whilst your son's school is well equipped with them. Your daughter's school has more science pupils per teacher than your son's school. You cannot bring a complaint against the governors of your daughter's school because she is in a single-sex school and cannot compare the facilities provided for her with those provided for boys in another school. But it *is* unlawful sex discrimination on the part of the local education authority because it is providing poorer facilities for female science students in its schools, and is, therefore, discriminating in the carrying out of its functions.

A local education authority has two single-sex schools in its area, one for girls and one for boys. The boys' school has places for 600 students, the girls' school for only 300 students. The local education authority is discriminating unlawfully by providing fewer places for girls than for boys.

In determining whether or not to award a discretionary grant, a local education authority must not use discriminatory criteria. Thus a local education authority which insists that applicants for a grant in an electronics engineering course must have had at least one year's work experience in the field may well be acting unlawfully because it is a field which women on the whole have not traditionally entered.

What can I do if I or my child has been discriminated against?

You can bring proceedings for sex discrimination in the County Court (see chapter 9).

If your complaint is about sex discrimination in the public sector of education – a state school or a special school, polytechnic or college maintained by the local education authority or funded by the Department of Education and Science – you must first of all give notice of it in writing to the Secretary of State for Education. The reasoning behind this is that, since the Secretary of State has ultimate responsibility for education in the public sector, he or she must first be given an opportunity to conduct inquiries and, if discrimination is found, to take steps to eradicate it. You cannot start proceedings unless either the Secretary of State has written to you and informed you that he or she does not require further time to consider the matter, or two months have passed since you first gave written notice. In a case relating to education in the public sector you must start proceedings within eight months of the act of discrimination taking place.

If the complaint is about a university or an independent school or college, you do not need to give notice to the Secretary of State, but must start proceedings within six months of the act of discrimination taking place.

Before deciding to start proceedings, write to the responsible body pointing out the discrimination and the fact that it is unlawful, and state that unless it is dealt with you intend to start proceedings. This may have the desired effect, and it will be quicker and easier than bringing proceedings in court.

If you feel that the discrimination against you is not an isolated incident, but indicative of the way in which a particular institution treats women in general, bring the matter to the attention of the Equal Opportunities Commission (for their address, see page 139). Write to them giving as much detail as you can. They have the resources and the powers in certain circumstances to conduct formal investigations, obtain information and make recommendations.

7: Housing and Premises

Is sex discrimination in housing unlawful?

Yes. Subject to certain exceptions, it is unlawful for owners of property or landlords or anyone authorized by them to sell or rent any property to discriminate against you if you are trying to acquire housing accommodation. It is also unlawful for owners or landlords or anyone who manages property for them to discriminate against you if you are already in occupation.

This chapter only deals with discrimination in the provision of housing accommodation. Discrimination in the provision of accommodation in hotels, hostels and boarding houses is dealt with in chapter 8, as is discrimination in obtaining a mortgage.

What about land and business premises?

Sex discrimination in the selling or renting of land and business premises is unlawful in the same way as discrimination in housing. However, as most problems arise in relation to housing, this chapter will concentrate on that aspect, although almost everything said here will apply equally to the disposal of land and business premises.

Does it make any difference whether I want to buy or rent the property?

No. The way in which you want to acquire the property is entirely irrelevant, as indeed is the size, quality and type of property. Sex discrimination is unlawful whether you are buying a freehold or a leasehold, or renting the property. Your tenancy could be a long one or a short one, or it could be for a fixed period or for an indefinite period requiring weekly or monthly payments of rent.

It is equally immaterial whether the property in question is a house, flat or a bed-sit. If, however, it is a bed-sit or a flat which is not self-contained (that is, you have to share certain amenities) and the landlord or his family live there as well, it may be classified as 'small premises' (see page 102). If that is the case, sex discrimination in respect of it will not be against the law.

It is also irrelevant if the property in question is not immediately available for occupation. Thus it is unlawful for property companies developing housing estates to discriminate in the selling of housing, even if they do so before the houses are complete and ready for occupation.

What is unlawful discrimination by owners and landlords?

It is unlawful for an owner or a landlord to discriminate against you on the grounds of your sex either by refusing to sell or rent you the property or by offering to do so on less favourable terms than those offered to men. In addition, it is unlawful for local authorities to discriminate on the grounds of sex in relation to any lists of persons in need of premises.

The landlord could be a private individual, a commercial organization, a local authority or a housing association. The landlord is also responsible for acts of discrimination by employees, unless he can show that such steps were taken as were reasonably practicable to stop the employee discriminating.

The following are examples of what would amount to unlawful sex discrimination:

You are a single woman and you go to see a house that was advertised for sale in a local newspaper. The owner shows you round the house, and then asks you whether you are buying it on your own or jointly with your husband. When you tell him that you are buying it on your own, he says that he would rather sell to a man because he has had problems in the past with women buyers pulling out at the last moment.

You go to see a landlord about renting a flat. You tell him that you are a teacher and earn £7,000 per annum. He offers to rent you the flat subject to you providing a suitable guarantor for the rent. You later discover that a male tenant in the same building, who is a clerk and earns £6,000 per annum, was not asked to provide a guarantor.

You want to purchase the long lease of a studio flat in a prestigious block in central London. The company which owns the property asks you to provide two references because they 'do not want the wrong kind of women in the block as this would lower the value of the whole block'. Male leaseholders are not asked to provide references.

Are there any circumstances in which landlords and owners can discriminate?

Yes, discrimination is allowed if it takes place in any of the following circumstances:

Owner-occupiers selling privately

An owner-occupier – that is someone who lives in the relevant house or flat and is either a freeholder or has a long lease in respect of it – can discriminate in disposing of it, as long as an estate agent is not employed to do so, and the sale is not advertised in any other way. If a 'for sale' sign is put up outside the property, then that sign is advertising its sale and, therefore, discrimination would be unlawful. This exception envisages a purely private transaction, and it is very unlikely that you would even know that it was taking place.

Small premises

A landlord can discriminate against you by refusing to sell or rent to you any premises if *all* the following three conditions are fulfilled:

(a) either the landlord or a 'near relative' of the landlord lives on the premises and intends to continue doing so. The term 'near relative' refers to the landlord's wife or husband, parent, child, grandparent, grandchild, brother or sister. It applies equally to half-brothers and half-sisters, illegitimate children and the spouses of illegitimate children;

(b) the landlord or a near relative has to share certain accommodation with the other people living there. The shared accommodation must be something other than a common entrance hall or staircase or storage accommodation. Thus it could be a kitchen, a bathroom or a lavatory;

(c) the premises are 'small premises'. This could mean either that the premises are divided in such a way as to provide accommodation for no more than three households, one of which is occupied by the landlord or near relative, or that there is accommodation on the premises for no more than six persons in addition to the landlord or near relative. The following examples show what this means:

The landlord's son lives in a flat on the ground floor. There are two flats on the first floor, one of which is occupied by two men, the other is vacant. All three flats share a bathroom. The landlord does not break the law if he or she refuses to rent the third flat to a woman.

The landlord's mother occupies two rooms in a large house. There are six rooms which are let to students. The landlord's mother shares a kitchen and a dining-room with the tenants. The landlord's refusal to let the rooms to any male students is lawful. If, however, there had been a seventh room in the house which could also be let, then his or her sex discrimination would have been unlawful because the house would no longer have counted as 'small premises'.

Voluntary bodies
Voluntary bodies, that is organizations which are not created by an Act of Parliament and are non-profit-making, are entitled to restrict their membership and the provision of benefits, facilities and services to members of one sex only. Thus it is lawful to have single-sex housing associations, and a man cannot complain of sex discrimination if a women's housing association refuses to provide him with accommodation.

Charitable housing trusts
If housing is provided by a charity, and the terms of the charitable instrument limit its provision to members of one sex only, then it does not break the law by doing so in order to give effect to the terms of the instrument (see page 127).

See also chapter 10 – General Exceptions.

What is unlawful discrimination by estate agents?
It is unlawful for agencies which are entrusted with the selling or renting of property to discriminate on the grounds of sex. A person who wants to sell his or her house or flat often uses an estate agent to find a buyer; similarly, a person wishing to let property often uses accommodation agencies or bureaux to find tenants.

It is unlawful for any of the above to discriminate against you by refusing to sell or rent the property to you, by offering to do so on less favourable terms than those that are offered to men, or by treating you less favourably in relation to lists of people in need of a particular type of premises. An estate agent would, therefore, be acting unlawfully if he kept separate lists of men and women looking for one-bedroomed flats to rent, and gave priority to the men when such accommodation became available. An estate agent also acts unlawfully if he asks female potential tenants to provide guarantors, but does not ask the male potential tenants to do so.

Agencies often discriminate because they have been instructed to do so by the landlord. If you decide to bring proceedings in such a case, ascertain who the landlord is and issue proceedings against the landlord as well as the estate agent. The landlord is equally responsible for anything the estate agent does with his or her authority.

If you work for an estate agent or accommodation bureau and you are instructed by a landlord to discriminate on the grounds of sex, you can report the landlord to the Equal Opportunities Commission (EOC). It is unlawful for the landlord to instruct you to discriminate in this way. This is something in respect of which individuals cannot take action, but the EOC can (see chapter 11).

Estate agents are, however, entitled to discriminate in circumstances in which landlords and owners can discriminate (see page 102), but the exception relating to owner-occupiers obviously does not apply in the case of estate agents.

What is unlawful discrimination when I am in occupation?

It is unlawful for anyone who manages the property in which you live to discriminate against you by refusing you or restricting your access to any of the benefits and facilities provided, by evicting you or by treating you less favourably than the male tenants in any way.

The manager of the property may be the landlord in person, or it may be property managers or managing agents. Large commercial landlords often delegate the day-to-day management of their properties to other companies. The landlord company, however, remains responsible for the actions of the property managers which are done with their authority, and in such a case you could bring proceedings against the landlord company as well as the property managers.

The following is an example of unlawful discrimination. A male tenant and a female tenant both fall into arrears with their rent. This is the first time that it has happened to either of them and the arrears are approximately the same. The landlord starts possession proceedings against the female tenant, but not against the male tenant.

What if the landlord does not allow me to sublet to a woman?

Most tenancies include a term about subletting. In some cases it is prohibited altogether – you are not allowed to sublet to anyone. In other cases, you are allowed to sublet provided that you get the consent of the landlord to do so. The landlord must not refuse consent unless there is reasonable justification for doing so (see *The Private Tenants Handbook* or *The Public Tenants Handbook* in this series).

If a landlord refuses consent because the proposed subtenant is a woman, this is unlawful sex discrimination against the woman. In such a case, there are two things which can be done. First, the prospective female subtenant can bring proceedings for sex discrimination against the landlord in the County Court. Second, you can apply to the County Court for an order declaring that the landlord's refusal to consent is unreasonable, and that you are allowed to sublet.

The same applies if you are assigning (transferring) your tenancy to someone else. People with long leases often regard themselves as the 'owners' of the property in question, and talk of 'buying' and 'selling' it. What you in fact do when you 'sell' the property is assign your long lease to someone else. Thus, if the freeholder (the landlord) refuses to consent to your selling (assigning) the premises to a woman, the landlord is unlawfully discriminating against the woman.

If the premises in question are 'small premises' and amenities have to be shared with the landlord or a member of the landlord's family (see page 102), the prospective sub-tenants or assignees cannot complain of sex discrimination. It is still, however, open to you as the tenant to seek a declaration that the consent is being unreasonably withheld.

What can I do if I have suffered discrimination in housing?

You can bring proceedings in the County Court against the discriminator. Proceedings must be started within six months of the act of discrimination taking place (see chapter 9 for details of how to bring and conduct proceedings in the County Court).

8: Goods, Facilities and Services

What are 'goods, facilities and services'?

In the preceding chapters we have dealt with discrimination in connection with your work (chapters 2, 3 and 4), your or your children's education (chapter 6) and your home (chapter 7). The other main area in which you are likely to suffer discrimination in everyday life will be in relation to the provision of 'goods, facilities and services'. This vague and general phrase covers almost everything you do in your daily life – things that you do for pleasure as well as things which have to be done out of necessity.

There is no special legal meaning attached to the words 'goods', 'facilities' and 'services'. They have the same meaning in this context as they do ordinarily. The meaning of 'goods' is obvious and needs no further elaboration. Providing 'facilities' simply means making available to you the opportunity to do something or to get some benefit. 'Services' are provided when work is done to meet some general needs.

What is unlawful discrimination in the provision of goods?

It is unlawful for anyone who is concerned with the provision of goods to the public, or to a section of it, to discriminate against you because of your sex either by not providing you with the goods or by treating you in some other way less favourably than the male customers.

Any shop (whether it is a showroom selling cars or a local greengrocer selling vegetables) is concerned with providing goods to the public. So indeed are market stalls and those who sell goods through mail-order catalogues. An example of someone providing goods to a section of the public is a wholesaler who sells only to retailers and not to the public at large.

It is very unlikely that any salesperson will discriminate against you by refusing to sell you their goods. Sex discrimination in this context usually occurs when a woman wants to buy goods on credit. The following are examples of unlawful sex discrimination:

A married woman goes into a department store to buy furniture. She puts down a deposit for part of the payment, and indicates that she wishes to pay the balance by means of a hire-purchase agreement. The shop assistant completes a hire-purchase document, without asking the woman any details about her earnings or savings. He then tells her that for her application to succeed her husband will have to sign a guarantee form. When she asks whether she would have been required to act as a guarantor if her husband had taken out the agreement, she is told that it would not have been necessary.

You arrange to buy goods on credit, but when the shop assistant discovers that you are in part-time employment, you are told that you are not entitled to apply for credit. The shop assistant explains that the company has a policy of refusing credit to all those in part-time employment, regardless of the individual's salary and the amount of credit requested. This would probably be indirect sex discrimination as the majority of part-time employees are women, and the requirement to be in full-time employment in order to qualify would exclude a larger percentage of women than of men.

What is unlawful discrimination in the provision of facilities?

It is unlawful for anyone who is concerned with providing facilities to the general public, or to a section of it, to discriminate against you on the grounds of your sex either by refusing to provide you with the facilities or by not providing you with facilities of the same quality, in the same manner and on the same terms as are normally provided to men. It is irrelevant whether the facilities are provided free or for payment.

The phrase 'provision of facilities' covers a wide range of activities in various spheres of your life, and it is impossible to give a complete list of all of them. The following are examples of facilities:

(a) access to and use of places which members of the public or a section of it are allowed to enter (such as parks, libraries and museums);

(b) accommodation in a hotel, boarding house or other similar establishment;

(c) facilities for entertainment, recreation or refreshment (such as cinemas, theatres, bingo halls, amusement arcades, swimming pools, sports centres, pubs, wine bars, restaurants, discotheques and night clubs);

(d) banking or insurance facilities, or the giving of grants, loans, credit or finance (this includes mortgages, overdraft facilities, home improvement loans and grants);

(e) facilities for transport or travel.

The following are examples of unlawful sex discrimination in the provision of facilities:

A wine bar refuses to serve women standing at the bar because it operates a 'house rule' which allows men customers to be served either at the bar or when seated at a table, whereas women customers are only served when seated at a table.

A publican excludes women from the use of entertainment facilities which are available to the male customers, such as snooker, pool or darts. A publican also breaks the law if he operates a bar exclusively for men (unless, of course, there is an equivalent women-only bar as well).

A single woman goes into a restaurant after midnight. The manager refuses to serve her. When asked for an explanation, he says that he has had problems in the past with prostitutes trying to attract custom in his restaurant and that he therefore prefers not to serve single women. He is quite prepared to serve a single man who comes into the restaurant on his own.

A discotheque charges £5 to admit men, but women are admitted free.

You and your husband apply to the building society for a mortgage. You are 26 years old and he is 28. You are both working and earn approximately the same amount. You have one child, and you make it clear to the building society that you do not intend to have any more. The building society says that in determining the amount of mortgage to give you, it will take into account your husband's earnings but not yours.

A man and a woman of similar financial standing and in similar employment both apply to the same bank for overdraft facilities of £1,000. The man is granted this facility, the woman is only allowed an overdraft of up to £300. Unless there is some good explanation for the different treatment, the bank has discriminated unlawfully.

What is unlawful discrimination in the provision of services?

It is unlawful for anyone concerned with the provision of services to the public, or to a section of it, (whether for payment or not) to discriminate against you because of your sex either by not providing you with the services or by providing you with services of inferior quality or on less favourable terms than they provide for men.

The following are examples of people concerned with the provision of services: people who provide 'professional' services, such as doctors, accountants, dentists, solicitors and surveyors; people who provide you with the skilled services of a trade, such as builders, carpenters, plumbers, electricians and car mechanics; and people who tend to your welfare needs, such as social workers, probation officers and health visitors.

What if the goods, facilities and services are provided abroad?

The general rule is that sex discrimination is only unlawful in relation to the provision of goods, facilities and services within Great Britain. There are, however, three exceptions to the general rule:

(a) sex discrimination in relation to the provision of travel facilities abroad is unlawful if the actual act of discrimination takes place in this country. Thus you can complain of discrimination if a travel agent in this country makes arrangements for your holiday which result in you being treated less favourably than your male counterparts when you are abroad;

(b) sex discrimination is unlawful if it takes place on board a British ship, aircraft or hovercraft, regardless of where the ship, aircraft or hovercraft is at the time of the incident;

(c) it is lawful to discriminate in the provision of banking or insurance facilities, or in the giving of grants, loans, credit or finance, where the facilities are for a purpose to be carried out, or in connection with risks wholly or mainly arising, outside Britain. Thus a bank in this country acts lawfully if it discriminates against a woman applying to the bank for a loan to develop property in Spain.

Is it ever lawful to discriminate in the provision of goods, facilities and services?

There is a large variety of circumstances in which discrimination is permitted by the law. Sex discrimination is lawful in the following cases:

Private clubs

Private clubs where entry to the club is regulated by the personal acceptability of the applicant to the existing members of the club. It is, therefore, lawful for gentlemen's clubs, such as the Garrick, and workingmen's clubs to discriminate against women by refusing to admit them or by treating them less favourably if they do admit them.

Political parties

Political parties are allowed to make special provisions for women in the constitution, organization or administration of the party. Thus a political party does not break the law if it has women's sections or organizes conferences for women only.

Voluntary bodies

Voluntary bodies (that is non-profit-making bodies not created by an Act of Parliament) are allowed to discriminate in two ways. First, they can restrict their membership to one sex only and limit the provision of any benefits, facilities and services to their members only (thus providing the benefits, etc to one sex only). Second, they can provide benefits for one sex only if that is the main object of the body. The following, therefore, are not breaking the law by not providing any benefits for men – homes for battered wives, hostels for single mothers and organizations providing legal advice to women only, such as Rights of Women.

Special care

Places established for persons needing special care, supervision or attention can restrict the provision of facilities and services to one sex only. This applies, for instance, to hospitals, reception centres provided by the Supplementary Benefits Commission, hostels for drug addicts, old people's homes and prisons.

Organized religion

A place which is occupied by or used for the purposes of an organized religion can restrict the provision of facilities and services to members of one sex only if it does so to comply with the doctrines of that religion or so as to avoid offending the religious susceptibilities of a significant number of its followers.

Decency and privacy

A place can restrict the provision of facilities and services to members of one sex only in order to perserve decency and privacy. This arises where the facilities or services are such that the presence of the opposite sex would cause serious embarrassment to the user, or the user is likely to be in a state of undress and might reasonably object to the presence of a member of the opposite sex, or if physical contact is likely between the user and any other person and that other person might reasonably object if the user is a member of the opposite sex. This would apply, for instance, to public lavatories, changing rooms, sauna baths and massage parlours.

Insurance

An insurance company or anyone selling life insurance, accident insurance or any other type of insurance which involves the assessment of risk is allowed to discriminate on the basis of statistical information if the following two factors are shown to exist. First, that the discrimination results from relying on statistical information which was obtained from a source on which it was reasonable to rely, and, second, that the discriminatory treatment was reasonable having regard to the statistics and to any other relevant factors.

For instance, an insurance company would be entitled to charge women more for health insurance than men if statistics showed that women were generally more prone than men to take time off work for sickness. Equally, it would be lawful to charge women lower premiums than men for life assurance if statistics showed that women tended to live longer than men.

Boarding houses

A person providing accommodation in a boarding house is entitled to discriminate if he or she or a near relative lives and intends to continue living on the premises, that person has to share certain amenities (other than storage accommodation or means of access) with the lodgers, and the premises cannot provide accommodation for more than six lodgers (see also page 102).

Charities

If a charitable instrument contains a provision for conferring benefits on members of one sex only, anything done to give effect to that provision is lawful. For instance, X creates a charitable trust to provide a home for single homeless women. The refusal to admit men to the home is lawful (see also page 127).

Communal accommodation

This refers to residential accommodation where either sleeping facilities are shared (such as in dormitories) or sanitary facilities (such as bathrooms and lavatories) are shared. It is lawful to limit the admission to this kind of accommodation to members of one sex only in order to preserve privacy and decency. If there are facilities or services which can only be provided effectively for people using the communal accommodation, it is lawful to exclude one sex from the facilities or services if they are also excluded from the accommodation. This would apply, for instance, to treatment at a health farm (see also page 129).

Special skills

If a particular skill is commonly exercised in a different way for men and women, it is lawful for the person exercising it to do so for members of one sex only. For example, it is lawful for a women's hairdresser to refuse to cut a man's hair.

A person who provides goods, facilities or services which are designed for one sex is not required to provide the corresponding goods, facilities and services for the opposite sex. Thus a shop selling women's clothes is not obliged to sell men's clothes as well.

See also chapter 10, General Exceptions.

What can I do if I have been discriminated against?

You can bring proceedings in the County Court, but must do so within six months of the act of discrimination taking place (see chapter 9 for proceedings in the County Court).

9: Proceedings in the County Court

When do I bring proceedings in the County court?
If you have suffered sex discrimination in education (see chapter 6), housing (see chapter 7) or the provision of goods, facilities and services (see chapter 8), you can start legal proceedings against the discriminator in a County Court.

In which County Court do I start proceedings?
England and Wales are divided into districts in each of which there is a County Court. There are some 340 County Courts altogether, located in the cities and other major centres of population. You must start proceedings in the County Court for the district in which the discriminator lives or carries on his business or in which the act of discrimination took place. If you are not certain as to the court in which you should start proceedings, inquire at the nearest County Court office. County Courts are usually listed in the telephone directory under 'Courts'.

Is there a time limit within which I must start proceedings?
If you are complaining about sex discrimination in public sector education (see page 98), you must start proceedings within eight months of the date on which the act of discrimination took place. In all other cases you must start proceedings within six months of the act of discrimination taking place. A month means a calendar month and in calculating the date on which the time limit expires remember to include the date on which the discrimination took place as the first day of the relevant period.

If you start proceedings after the expiry of the time

limit, the court may still hear your case if, in all the circumstances of the case, it considers that it is just and equitable to do so (see page 67 for the circumstances in which it may be just and equitable to extend the time limit).

Can I get more information before deciding whether or not to start proceedings?

Yes, you are entitled to ask the discriminator questions about the way in which he has treated you, his reasons for that treatment and any other questions which may be relevant. There is a standard form available free of charge from the EOC, which you can use for the purpose of asking the questions. You do not have to use this form and can ask the questions in a letter if you wish to. You may, however, find it a lot simpler to use the standard form.

If you send the questionnaire to the discriminator *before* starting proceedings and within the time limit for starting proceedings, then your questions and his replies become evidence in the case, and you can rely upon them in court. If he does not reply to your questions within a reasonable time, or his answers are vague or evasive, the court is entitled to infer that he has unlawfully discriminated against you.

If you have already started proceedings you can only serve questions upon the discriminator if the court gives you leave to do so. If it does give you leave and you serve the questions within the period it specifies, then the questions and replies will be admissible as evidence.

The type of question you ask will of course depend upon the facts of your particular case. If you are not certain about what questions to ask or how to formulate them, seek assistance before doing so.

It is always useful to ask the questions before starting proceedings because it gives you a good indication of the strength of your case which may be an important consideration in deciding whether or not to pursue it.

Can I get legal aid?

Yes, but in order to do so, you must:

(a) convince the Law Society that it is reasonable for you to bring the proceedings. This essentially means that your case must be strong enough to merit it. If you have a weak or hopeless case, it is unlikely that you will get legal aid; *and*

(b) fulfil the financial requirements. Your income and capital must be below a certain level for you to qualify for legal aid.

You can get legal aid forms from solicitors, law centres, CABs (Citizens' Advice Bureaux), or the nearest Law Society's legal aid area office. The forms are fairly complicated to fill in, so if you don't have a solicitor get someone at the law centre or the CAB to help you fill it in. If you don't know which solicitor you want to act for you, ask the law centre or CAB for their advice. They will know of solicitors who do legal aid work and possibly those who have some experience and expertise in the field of sex discrimination.

After the forms have been sent, you will probably be called for an interview by the Department of Social Security. It is their function to assess your financial situation and tell the Law Society the maximum which you can afford to pay. It is important to attend this interview as failure to do so may result in you losing your right to legal aid.

Depending on your financial circumstances you might get legal aid with 'nil contribution' (that is, you won't have to pay anything towards your costs), you may not get legal aid at all or you may get legal aid subject to you paying a certain contribution towards it.

Legal aid will cover all the expenses of having a

solicitor prepare your case and of having a solicitor or barrister represent you at the hearing itself.

If you are refused legal aid on the ground that your case does not merit it, you can appeal to the legal aid area committee.

For more information on legal aid, see *The Lawyer–Client Handbook* in this series.

Can I get legal advice or assistance from anywhere else?

There are a number of bodies which can provide you with advice, assistance and, in some cases, representation at court, without charging you anything.

The EOC

See pages 70–1 for the circumstances in which the EOC will provide assistance, and the ways in which it can assist you.

Law centres

See page 71.

Citizens' Advice Bureaux

See page 71.

Solicitors

See page 72.

How are proceedings started in the County Court?

You start proceedings by delivering to the appropriate County Court a request for a summons and two copies of your 'particulars of claim'. The 'request' is a form which you fill in so that the court can prepare a document called a 'summons' which is served on the discriminator, and tells him about your claim and what he has to do.

The 'particulars of claim' is a document which sets out

briefly the facts of your case and the remedy which you are seeking from the court. Although this sounds relatively simple, there is a certain legal and technical formula for drafting a 'particulars of claim', and it is generally better to get a lawyer to draft it for you.

The other side then files a document known as the 'defence' which sets out in essence the facts on which they intend to rely in order to resist your claim. Either side is entitled to ask the other to elaborate on and clarify matters stated in their respective documents. These questions are contained in a document known as a 'request for further and better particulars'.

All the documents mentioned above are known collectively as 'pleadings'. It is important that they should be an accurate summary of the facts on which you rely, and as they are normally written in a formal legalistic style, it is far better to leave it to lawyers to prepare them.

Who decides a case in the County Court?

A case in the County Court is heard and decided by a judge. The judge may summon to sit with and assist him one or more persons who have skill and experience in the matter to which the proceedings relate. These persons are known as 'assessors'. They are, however, merely advisers to the judge, and the decision is ultimately made by the judge alone according to his opinion of the law and the merits of the case.

Can I conduct a case myself?

Proceedings in a County Court are much more formal than in an industrial tribunal, and you will find it very difficult, if not impossible, to prepare and present your case without the services of a lawyer.

It has already been pointed out that certain formal documents have to be prepared before the case comes to court, and the difficulty of preparing these without the assistance of a lawyer (see page 120).

The procedure at the hearing itself is very formal and the rules of evidence are strictly adhered to. There are precise rules about evidence which is admissible and that which isn't, and it is very unlikely that a non-lawyer will be familiar with these. You will, therefore, be at a considerable disadvantage if you are conducting your own case.

If you do decide to conduct your own case, the following are a few useful tips:

Have ready any document which is relevant and assists your case. Prepare two extra copies of all documents – one for the other side and one for the judge.

You are entitled to see and inspect any documents which the other side has in its possession and which are relevant to your case. If you have difficulty in getting these documents from the other side, you can apply to a Registrar for discovery (for discovery, see page 72).

Make sure that all your witnesses are willing to attend, and are available for the date of the hearing.

Arrive at court in time for the hearing. If you cannot attend for any reason, for instance because you are ill, let the court know in advance.

The procedure in the court as to opening your case, giving evidence, cross-examination and closing speeches is the same as in the industrial tribunal, except that it is more formal (see page 76 for procedure in the industrial tribunal).

Will I have to pay the other side's costs if I lose?

The general rule in the County Court is that the loser pays all the winner's costs. There are, however, two situations in which you won't have to pay the other side's costs if you lose. First, if you are assisted by the EOC and they have provided you with representation, they will pay the other side's costs. Secondly, if you were granted legal aid with 'nil contribution' it is extremely unlikely that the court would order you to pay the winner's costs. If, however, legal aid was granted subject to you paying a certain contribution, then you may be ordered to pay the same amount as your contribution towards the other side's costs.

If the discriminator has engaged a solicitor and a barrister, it is likely that his costs will be quite substantial. Therefore, if you have not been granted legal aid and the EOC has refused your application for assistance, think long and hard before starting proceedings. Take advice from a law centre, a CAB or a solicitor (on the green form scheme) on your prospects of succeeding before deciding whether or not to go ahead.

In what circumstances should I settle a case?
The same considerations apply when settling a case in the County Court as do in the industrial tribunal (see page 74). The only additional factor, and it is an important one, is the question of costs. If there is a risk that you may lose the case, and therefore be ordered to pay the other side's costs, it would probably be advisable to accept a settlement. If at all possible try to get the other side to accept paying your costs as part of the settlement.

How do I prove discrimination?
As you are the person bringing the case you have to satisfy the court on a balance of probabilities that you were discriminated against because of your sex. 'On a balance of probabilities' simply means that it is 'more probable than not'.

Discrimination in a County Court is proved in exactly the same way as in an industrial tribunal – the court takes an identical approach to the tribunal in reaching its decision (see pages 77–81).

What orders can the court make if I win?

In addition to declaring that the person in question has unlawfully discriminated against you, the court may order one or both of the following:

(a) an injunction to stop him from discriminating unlawfully in the future. An injunction is an order of the court, and if the person disobeys it he can be fined or imprisoned for contempt of court. Although injunctions are usually asked for in the Particulars of Claim, they are not often granted by courts in discrimination cases;

(b) damages. This is monetary compensation for any financial loss that you have actually suffered or are likely to suffer in the future. In addition, the court can compensate you for injury to your feelings. In most cases, the only damages you receive are for injury to feelings. The sum awarded for this varies according to the circumstances of your case and from court to court, but the average amount given nowadays is about £200–£300. If the case is one of indirect discrimination, no damages will be awarded if the discriminator proves that the requirement or condition was not applied with the intention of discriminating on the grounds of sex.

If you have incurred any costs in bringing the case, the court will order the other side to pay these. This would cover lawyers' fees (if you engaged any), court fees (you have to pay a certain amount for starting proceedings), witness expenses and any other expenses which you have reasonably incurred in bringing proceedings. If you were assisted by the EOC, then you won't receive any costs because you will not have incurred any expenses. Any costs awarded will go to the EOC, who will use it to pay your legal representation.

Can I appeal if I lose?

You can appeal to the Court of Appeal only if the judge misdirected himself on the law or if there was no evidence to support his findings of fact. A notice of appeal must be lodged within four weeks of the date on which judgment was given.

10: General Exceptions

What are 'general exceptions'?

In the preceding chapters we have looked at conduct which is unlawful in various spheres of your life – in relation to your work, education, housing, and the provision of goods, facilities and services. In each category, there were certain exceptions, that is circumstances in which discrimination was permitted.

In addition there are other exceptions which do not fall into any specific category but apply to all the areas we have considered. These have been put together in this chapter and called 'general exceptions'. In some cases the extent to which discrimination is permitted is limited, in others it is not and a general licence to discriminate is given.

The exceptions are broadly divided into the following five categories:

(a) charities;
(b) sport;
(c) communal accommodation;
(d) acts done under statutory authority;
(e) acts safeguarding national security.

We shall look at each of these in closer detail in the rest of this chapter. If a discriminator defends your claim of discrimination against him on the basis that the incident falls within one of these categories, then it is upon him to prove that it does.

What is a 'charity'?

A charity is an institution or a trust which was set up to carry out purposes which are exclusively charitable. There is no exhaustive list of charitable purposes but it covers such things as the relief of poverty, advancement of education or religion, promotion of health, provision of recreational facilities and other purposes which are generally beneficial to the community. The benefits of the charity should be available to the public or to a section of it. There is a central register of charities which is open to public inspection.

When rich people die, they often leave their assets in a will or a trust for some specific charitable purpose. Thus institutions such as schools, hospitals, colleges and homes for the elderly or disabled are often set up and/or funded out of these assets. It is essential that the assets are used in such a way that they comply with the wishes of the person who gave them.

To what extent are charities allowed to discriminate?

Charities are allowed to discriminate by conferring benefits on members of one sex only. The benefits may relate to education, accommodation or the provision of some other facilities or services. Anyone who discriminates in order to give effect to a charitable instrument acts lawfully. In the case of educational trusts whose benefits are confined to members of one sex only, it is open to the trustees to apply to the Education Minister to offer those benefits to both sexes.

The following actions, for instance, are lawful if they are being done to give effect to the provisions of a charitable instrument:

The giving of scholarships to women studying medicine.

The setting up of a nursing home for elderly men.

The setting up of a hostel for young unmarried mothers.

If, however, a charitable trust provides for the setting up of an old people's home, then the trustees act unlawfully if they discriminate against the members of one sex either by refusing to admit them or treating them less favourably in the home, because nothing in the charitable instrument provides for it.

How is discrimination lawful in sport?

It is lawful to limit the participation in any competitive sport to members of one sex only where the physical strength, stamina or physique of the average woman puts her at a disadvantage to the average man. For example, it is lawful to have separate athletics events (such as running, long jump, high jump, javelin throwing) for men and women. It would not, however, be lawful to exclude women from competitive events in which their physical strength or stamina play no part, such as, for instance, darts and pool.

What is 'communal accommodation'?

'Communal accommodation' means either:

(a) residential accommodation which includes dormitories or other shared sleeping accommodation which for reasons of privacy or decency should be used by members of one sex only; or

(b) residential accommodation all or part of which should be used by members of one sex only because of the nature of the sanitary facilities (that is, bathrooms and lavatories) serving the accommodation.

What is lawful discrimination in relation to communal accommodation?

It is lawful to discriminate as regards admission to communal accommodation (that is, to admit members of one sex only) provided that the accommodation is managed in such a way that men and women are treated as fairly and equitably as circumstances permit. In deciding whether the accommodation is managed in such a way, the courts or tribunals will take account of whether and how far it is reasonable to expect the accommodation to be altered or extended, or additional accommodation to be provided so as to cater more equally for the sexes, and also the frequency of the respective demands and needs of the sexes for the accommodation.

Furthermore, it is lawful to discriminate in the provision of a benefit, facility or service to members of one sex only if such a benefit, etc. can only be provided to persons using the communal accommodation. This would apply, for instance, to treatment at a health farm. Such discrimination is, however, only lawful if the benefit, facility or service in question cannot *properly and effectively* be provided except to persons using the communal accommodation.

In the employment context, however, discrimination in the admission to communal accommodation and in the provision of benefits, facilities and services which can only be provided to the users of the accommodation is only lawful if the person providing it makes such arrangements as are reasonably practicable to compensate those members of the sex to whom the accommodation or the benefits, etc. have been refused. For example, one of the perks provided in your job is a free week at a health farm. However, the health farm with which your employer has an arrangement is for men only. Your employer would only be acting lawfully if he made arrangements for female employees to attend another health farm, or provided them with the money to attend another health farm for a week.

What are 'acts done under statutory authority'?

Anything which is done in order to comply with the requirements of an Act of Parliament or of an instrument made or approved by Parliament under such an Act is an act done under statutory authority.

Is it lawful to discriminate to comply with the requirements of an Act of Parliament?

Any sex discrimination which results from following the provisions of an Act of Parliament passed before 12 November 1975, or of any instrument made or approved by Parliament under such an Act, is lawful. It is quite likely, however, that any such discrimination may be against EEC law.

What kind of discrimination is permitted to safeguard national security?

If 'national security' is involved, discrimination is permitted in every sphere of your life. If the discrimination is *not* in relation to employment, all that is required is a certificate signed by or on behalf of a Government Minister certifying that an act was done for the purpose of safeguarding national security. No one is entitled to look behind the certificate and inquire as to why a certain act was necessary to safeguard national security. The Minister's certificate is conclusive evidence of the fact that it was.

The position in relation to employment is different. It is not open to a Minister to issue a conclusive certificate, and the tribunal will look at the arguments put forward by the employer and decide whether sex discrimination was necessary in order to safeguard national security.

It is difficult, however, to see how an act of sex discrimination could ever be necessary to safeguard national security.

11: Other Unlawful Acts of Discrimination

Are there any other acts of discrimination which are unlawful?

We have so far looked at sex discrimination which can have a direct effect on you, and the legal action which you can take if you are the victim of such discrimination. In addition, there are other acts of discrimination which do not necessarily have an identifiable victim but are nevertheless unlawful. These are acts in respect of which you as an individual cannot bring any legal proceedings. It is, however, open to the Equal Opportunities Commission (EOC) to take legal action in respect of them.

The acts referred to above are:

(a) discriminatory advertisements;
(b) instructions to discriminate;
(c) pressure to discriminate;
(d) discriminatory practices; and
(e) persistent discrimination.

The rest of this chapter explains more fully these unlawful acts, and the action that can be taken in respect of them.

What is unlawful discrimination in advertising?

It is unlawful for anyone to publish, or place for publication, an advertisement which indicates, or might reasonably be taken to indicate, an intention to do an act which is, or might be, unlawful discrimination (chapters 3, 4, 6, 7 and 8 describe acts of discrimination which are unlawful in various spheres of your life).

It is completely irrelevant where the advertisement appears. It could be in a newspaper, magazine or some other publication; it could be broadcast on television or radio; it could be displayed on a notice, sign or show-card; it could be in circulars or catalogues or any other material which is distributed. Nor does it matter that the advertisement will not be seen by the general public, but only by a select number of people. Thus discriminatory advertising in an in-house magazine, brought out by a company just for its staff, is unlawful.

If an advertisement uses a job description with a sexual connotation (such as 'waiter', 'salesgirl', 'postman' or 'stewardess'), it will be taken to indicate an intention to discriminate (and thus be unlawful), unless the advertisement contains something to show that that is not the intention. For example, an advertisement which reads 'Waiters required for famous West End restaurant. Salary £7,500 p.a. Experience preferred but not necessary. Apply Box No. 112,' would be unlawful because there is nothing in it to indicate that the job is open to women as well as men.

If, however, the above advertisement had read 'Waiters and Waitresses required for famous West End restaurant', or had contained the words. 'Male and female applicants will be considered for the job' at the end, it would be lawful in spite of the use of the word 'waiters', because it would clearly indicate an intention *not* to discriminate.

It must be remembered, of course, that the discriminatory advertisement is only unlawful if the intended act of discrimination is itself unlawful. Therefore, if the law allows discrimination in certain circumstances, advertising to that effect is also lawful. For example, an employer is allowed to employ men only for a job if being a man is a genuine occupational qualification for the job (see page 40). In such circumstances it would be lawful to advertise for men only for the job. Thus an advertisement which read 'Male attendants wanted for men's lavatories' would not be against the law. Similarly, a landlord is allowed to discriminate if accommodation is to be provided in what are known as 'small premises' (see page 102). In such a case, an advertisement for male tenants only would be lawful.

The following are examples of unlawful discriminatory advertisements:

'Small PR firm looking for secretaries. Ideal opportunities for intelligent lively girls who have initiative and ambition. Apply to . . .'

'Clerical staff needed. Applicants must be under 30 and have experience in using word processors. Apply to . . .' This advertisement may be unlawful as the age requirement would indirectly discriminate against women (see page 5).

Proceedings in respect of a discriminatory advertisement can be brought against both the person who placed the advertisement and the person who published it. The publisher may, however, have a defence if he can prove that,

(a) he relied on a statement made by the person placing the advertisement that it would not be unlawful because the intended act was not unlawful, and

(b) that it was reasonable for him to rely on that statement.

It is a criminal offence for anyone placing an advertisement knowingly or recklessly to mislead the publisher as to its lawfulness. Anyone who does so may be brought before a magistrates' court and, if convicted, be fined up to £400.

What can I do if I see a discriminatory advertisement?

Report the matter at once to the Equal Opportunities Commission (EOC), giving as much detail of the advertisement as possible. If it appeared in a newspaper or magazine, send them a cutting of it with details of the name of the publication and the issue in which it appeared. If you saw the advertisement somewhere else, give as much detail as possible about its contents and about where and when you saw it. Remember to do this as soon as possible, because if the EOC are to take any proceedings in court in respect of it they must do so within six months of the advertisement appearing.

What are unlawful instructions to discriminate?

It is unlawful for someone who has authority over you or a special relationship with you whereby you normally do what they ask, to tell you to do anything which would amount to unlawful discrimination as described in chapters 3–4 and 6–8. The actual words used by the person do not matter; it is irrelevant whether they amount to a formal command, a request or the simple expression of a preference. What matters is the course of action which they are designed to bring about. If the result is going to be unlawful discrimination, then the instruction to you is unlawful.

The following examples show the kind of instruction which is unlawful:

A restaurant advertises for waiters and waitresses. The owner of the restaurant tells the manager not to hire any women who have young children because, in his experience, they are extremely unreliable employees. The owner's instructions to the manager are unlawful even if, in the event, no women with young children apply for the job.

A company asks an employment agency to find a driver for one of their directors. The agency sends a woman to be interviewed for the post. On seeing her, the director calls the agency and says that he doesn't want a woman driver, and could they please send him a man instead. That is an unlawful instruction.

What is unlawful pressure in discrimination?

It is unlawful for anyone to bring pressure to bear on another person to discriminate unlawfully in any of the ways described in chapters 3–4 and 6–8. The person bringing pressure to bear on you may try to exert influence over you or persuade you, either by offering you some benefit if you do as he says, or by threatening to do something to you if you do not do as he says. It is unlawful regardless of the form that it takes. It is unlawful even if the offer of a benefit or threat is not made directly to you, but is made in such a way that you are likely to hear of it. The following are examples of unlawful pressure in discrimination:

A managing director's advances towards a female employee are rejected by her. When the question of promotion arises, the managing director speaks to her immediate superior and tells him that it would be in his interest to make sure that she is not promoted, although she is the most suitable candidate. The managing director is breaking the law by putting pressure on the immediate superior to discriminate unlawfully against the woman.

A golf club appoints a woman golfer as a professional (to coach beginners). Certain male members take exception to her appointment and start putting the word about that the current chairman of the club will not be re-elected unless the woman is sacked. Their conduct remains unlawful even if they do not say this directly to the chairman but do so in such a way that it is likely that he will come to hear of it.

What can I do if someone instructs or pressurizes me to discriminate?

Report the matter at once to the Equal Opportunities Commission (EOC), giving as much detail as you can about what was said to you, by whom, and when. Remember the EOC has only six months within which to bring proceedings.

If you lose your job because you reported an unlawful instruction or inducement to the EOC, you can bring proceedings in the industrial tribunal against you employers on the grounds that you have been vicitimized (see page 13).

What action can the Equal Opportunities Commission (EOC) take?
If the EOC has evidence about discriminatory advertising or instructions or pressure to discriminate, they can bring legal proceedings against the person responsible.

If the advertising, pressure or instructions relate to employment (that is, any of the matters contained in chapters 3 and 4), the EOC will first of all apply to the industrial tribunal to decide whether an unlawful act of discrimination has taken place. If the tribunal decides that it has and it appears to the EOC that the person in question is likely to do the same thing again, the EOC can apply to the County Court for an injunction (a court order) to stop him doing so.

If the advertising, pressure or instructions are in relation to any other matter, the EOC can bring proceedings in the County Court. They can apply for one of two things. First, they can ask the court to give a ruling that the person concerned behaved unlawfully by publishing or causing to be published a discriminatory advertisement, or by instructing or pressurizing someone else to discriminate. Second, if they are of the view that the person concerned has broken the law by doing one of the above and that it is likely that he will do so again, they can ask the court to grant an injunction to stop the person from breaking the law in the same way in the future.

If a person disobeys an injunction, he can be brought back before the court for contempt, and can be fined and/or imprisoned.

What is a discriminatory practice and what can be done about it?

A 'discriminatory practice' is when someone imposes a condition or requirement which, if implemented, would result in indirect discrimination against women or, in the employment related field, against married persons (for indirect discrimination see pages 5–7). The condition or requirement has, however, been so effective as a deterrent that there is no actual victim of indirect discrimination because no woman (or married person) has ever applied for the job or benefit in question.

For example, an employer states that all job applicants for a clerical post must be under 30. This age requirement, if implemented, would result in indirect discrimination against women. However, no woman under the age of 30 bothers applying for the job because she feels that she will not be considered for it. A woman cannot complain about the age requirement unless she applies for the job and is turned down.

If you know of anyone who is imposing a discriminatory condition or requirement, report the matter to the EOC. They can conduct a formal investigation and, if satisfied that a discriminatory practice is being operated, they can serve a 'non-discrimination notice' on the person. This will essentially tell that person not to impose the discriminatory condition or requirement. If the notice is not complied with, the EOC can take legal proceedings and obtain an injunction (court order) to stop the condition or requirement from continuing to be imposed.

Is there anything to stop a person who has lost a case from discriminating again?

If you bring a case in the industrial tribunal (for sex discrimination or under the Equal Pay Act) or the County Court and win, but suspect or know that the person will continue to discriminate or pay different wages to men and women, report the matter to the EOC.

You personally cannot take any legal proceedings to stop this person discriminating in the future, but the EOC can. If at any time within five years of you winning your case it appears to the EOC that the discriminator will continue to break the law, they can apply to the County court for an injunction (a court order) restraining them from doing so.

12: Equal Opportunities Commission

What is the Equal Opportunities Commission?

The Equal Opportunities Commission (EOC) was set up in 1975 and it has the following duties:

(a) to work towards the elimination of discrimination;

(b) to promote equality of opportunity between men and women generally; and

(c) to keep under review the workings of the Sex Discrimination Act 1975 and the Equal Pay Act 1970 and to recommend amendments where necessary.

The EOC should consist of at least eight but not more than fifteen Commissioners, all of whom are appointed by the Secretary of State either on a full-time or part-time basis. One of these is then appointed by the Secretary of State to be the chairperson of the EOC, and one or two others are appointed to be deputy chairperson(s). In 1988 there were fourteen Commissioners, including a full-time chairperson and a part-time deputy chairperson.

The EOC is funded entirely by the Home Office. Its grant for 1988 amounted to £3,810,000. At the end of 1988 it had 179 members of staff, 139 of whom were women.

The EOC's main office is in Manchester at Overseas House, Quay Street, Manchester M3 3HN (telephone 061-833-9244). In addition it has regional offices in Wales and Scotland. The office in Wales is at Caerwys House, Windsor Lane, Cardiff CF1 1LB (telephone 0222-43552) and the one in Scotland is at St Andrews House, 141 West Nile Street, Glasgow G1 2RN (telephone 041-332-8018). There is also a press office in London at 1 Bedford Street, London WC2 (telephone 01-379-6323).

Notes